the doorway, facing

A

B

C

G

H

nose, 26·1 cms

...tie of the Behisun, 60·cms

Cms

of Radius, 20·cms

Cms 16·6 cms

TUTANKHAMUN

EXCAVATING THE ARCHIVE
TUTANKHAMUN

THE GRIFFITH INSTITUTE

BODLEIAN
LIBRARY
PUBLISHING

CONTENTS

For James Ivory

Every day I unbury – I dig up. I find relics of myself in the sand that women made thousands of years ago, when I heard songs by the Nile.

Virginia Woolf, *The Waves*, 1931

The tomb of Tutankhamun is one of the most famous discoveries in modern archaeology, but the historical reality of both the burial and its excavation by Howard Carter is not as straightforward as people often assume. Carter's archive was donated to the Griffith Institute in Oxford by his niece Phyllis Walker in the 1940s, and it reveals something of the complexities of the tomb's histories, both ancient and modern. The archive itself is, like the tomb and excavation, the result of multiple, interconnected historical processes. This small book celebrates and commemorates this cultural resource with an anthology of fifty items. From a modern perspective, it is easy either to glorify or to vilify the English excavator and his team, but the archive can help to contextualize events within their cultural and historical setting, and to enable a nuanced assessment.

The items in this book are selected and described by staff of the Griffith Institute, Elizabeth Fleming and Francisco Bosch-Puche, with some entries by Cat Warsi and by Jenni Navratil, who was also responsible for the imaging. The selection is a personal one based on the staff's experience both of the archive and of the questions posed by researchers and visitors; many other choices are possible. I, as editor, have shaped these entries, casting them into a single voice. Although it has been a very collaborative effort, the responsibility for the particular interpretations offered here remains the editor's. We have tried to convey the archive's ability to engage and inform those who consult it, and the chosen items are a mixture of the iconic and the less familiar. Whenever these images show objects from the tomb, we have noted the objects' dimensions as they are recorded in the archive, unless a human scale is visible. Each item is accompanied by its archival details.

We are deeply indebted to former staff of the Griffith Institute, including Melissa Downing, Alison Hobby, Sue Hutchison, Vincent Razanajao, Anne-Claire Salmas, Cat Warsi and, in particular, Jaromir Malek. Among earlier

PREFACE

generations, we particularly remember Diana Magee, Helen Murray and
Fiona Strachan. We also want to express our deepest gratitude to the families
and descendants of the Tutankhamun excavation team: it is their generous
donation of original documentation, including personal family papers, that
has made the archive possible. Thanks are also due to the members of the
Griffith Institute management committee, to the institute's most recent
directors Elizabeth Frood and Maren Schentuleit, and to Daniela Rosenow
as project officer for the exhibition; and also to the various volunteers and
conservators, past and present, who have worked on the archival material,
and the funding bodies whose grants have allowed the archive to make new
acquisitions. We are more than grateful to Marianne Eaton-Krauss for reading
and improving the text of this book; to Heba Abd el-Gawad for generously
discussing the Introduction; and to Henrietta McCall for invaluable help with
editing our narratives.

We are very grateful to the Bodleian Library Publishing and exhibition
staff, especially Samuel Fanous, Susie Foster, Sallyanne Gilchrist, Dot Little,
Janet Phillips, Leanda Shrimpton and Madeline Slaven; to The Queen's
College; to Liam McNamara and Paul Collins at the Ashmolean Museum;
to Eleanor Dobson for advice on the modern reception of the discovery; and
to Fatma Keshk and Hebatallah Ibrahim for assistance with Arabic sources.
In Oxford Humanities we owe much to the support of Karen O'Brien and
Victoria McGuinness, and at the Oriental Institute to Ulrike Roesler, Thomas
Hall and Emily Bush. Use of external images was kindly enabled by Alaa
Awad, Peter Clark, Anthony Roth Costanzo and Adam Lowe.

We are grateful to the archive's many visitors and researchers over the
years, who have shared and supported our curation for these records, and
whose work has established friendships across national boundaries and, above
all, with Egypt.

R.B. Parkinson

4

INTRODUCTION
THE 'WONDERFUL' THINGS

R.B. PARKINSON

A FUNERAL

On a spring day towards the end of the fourteenth century BCE a group of officials repeatedly pressed seals into mud plaster on a wall, covering it with the names of King Tutankhamun, and closing up the small rock-cut tomb where they had placed the funerary equipment of that young man, less than twenty years old, whose death had been so unexpected. Over the previous days, at the end of long and complex ceremonies, they had deposited his mummified body in its golden coffins, erected shrines around it and walled up the burial chamber. Then they had placed items used in the ceremonies in the other rooms, which were already partially filled with equipment deposited earlier. Once the outer entrance was walled up and sealed, the officials climbed the short flight of steps back up into the open air of the desert valley (Figure 1).[1]

Exactly how or when this all happened is not recorded, but it certainly was not a simple process. Some of the king's funerary equipment had been appropriated from his predecessors' burials, and the workers in the tomb left behind traces of haste and changes of plan: it had even been necessary to cut away some of the steps and enlarge the doorway to get the shrines inside the tomb. Their supposedly final closure of the burial was itself not a clean ending: soon afterwards intruders entered the tomb (perhaps even twice) intending to rob it. The officials later tidied up the disorder left by the robbers and resealed the doorways, with the king's body still safe and undisturbed. Traces of all these unplanned activities survived, including even finger marks left inside ointment vessels as someone pilfered the contents (Figure 2).

These officials would have watched Tutankhamun grow into a young man, having ascended the throne as a boy after a period of cultural turmoil when his (probable) father Akhenaten had closed the temples in favour of a new god. Monuments proclaimed the young king's glorious restoration of

The objects lay quiet for thousands of years.

E.M. FORSTER, *Abinger Harvest*, 1936

Figure 1 A section of the wall closing the tomb entrance (Carter no. 4); the mud plaster is stamped with the official seal of the royal necropolis. Burton P0277.

11

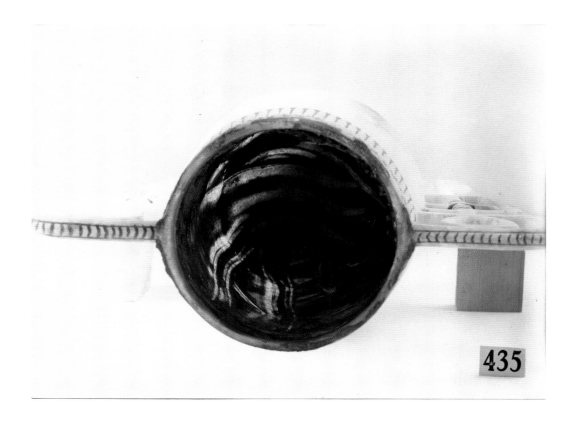

435

Figure 2 Ancient finger traces left by someone who removed most of the ointment from a calcite jar in the tomb (Carter no. 435). Burton P1653.

the traditional temples, whose 'sanctuaries were as if they had never existed … the land was in distress, and the gods had turned away from this land'.[2] Nevertheless, the following dynasties were to write Tutankhamun out of these records along with his heretic father. Some more intimate memories survive in the objects the officials deposited – personal donations of ritual equipment by well-known court dignitaries, small-scale furniture made for the child king, a white wooden box for shaving equipment labelled in ink as 'the kit of his Majesty (life, prosperity, health!) when he was a boy', a walking cane inscribed with 'a reed which his Majesty chose and cut with his own hand from a clump of reeds', a lock of his grandmother's hair and, most poignantly, the two mummified bodies of his prematurely born (and unnamed) daughters.[3] The objects in the tomb would give clues about his life to later generations, and they would one day be seen by millions across the world, but for the moment they were securely stored away. For the officials and workers in the burial ground of kings, there was probably a sense of relief that a long, complex and very awkward task had been completed.

DISCOVERY

The steps leading down to the sealed door were uncovered again on
4 November 1922 by the skilled Egyptian workforce employed by the English
excavator Howard Carter (1874–1939). Carter had been trained as an artist
and had moved into excavating without any formal academic qualifications.
It cannot have been at all easy for him, as the son of a Norfolk illustrator and
artist, to pursue his career in a society dominated by the upper classes, and

Figure 3 A portrait of the archaeologist as an English
gentleman: Howard Carter by his brother William
Carter in 1924. This portrait hung in Carter's London flat
and now hangs in the Griffith Institute Archive. Carter
MSS viii.2.

he later acquired the reputation of being a difficult person to work with, obstinate and 'quite impossible' (Figure 3).[4] In 1899 the French director-general of the Antiquities Service of Egypt, Gaston Maspero (1846–1916), appointed him as the first 'chief inspector of antiquities' in Upper Egypt, but after 1909 Carter worked independently, funded by the amateur Egyptologist and aristocrat George Edward Stanhope Molyneux Herbert, 5th earl of Carnarvon (1866–1923). As Carter later narrated it, the tomb was discovered just as Carnarvon's patience with a lack of major discoveries was running out.

The tomb of Tutankhamun has been described as 'the greatest find ever made'[5] and its contents have been celebrated as spectacular 'treasures' in blockbuster touring exhibitions. Although the tomb was small and had been hastily repurposed for the king, it was filled with artefacts in a sophisticated style of court art from a rich imperial age (Figure 4), and it was the only royal burial to survive (substantially) intact from ancient Egypt. The modern clearing and recording of the tomb were highly contingent processes, shaped by many chance factors, just as the ancient deposition had been: it took a full ten years of work, characterized by various tensions and disputes, both personal and political. The later official accounts are partial: Carter and Carnarvon undoubtedly investigated more of the tomb on their first entry than Carter later admitted. They had expected to retain some of their 'finds' under the old colonialist regulations, established by the French-run Antiquities Service in the late nineteenth century, which allowed foreign excavators to keep a share of excavated objects. Since 1914, Egypt had been occupied as a British protectorate. Even before independence was finally achieved in February 1922, voices such as E.M. Forster's (1879–1970) were raised against the nationalistic manner in which antiquities were collected by Europe.[6] It was clear that the old colonial system was indefensible. The contents of an intact royal tomb were too important to be divided and exported, and the newly independent Egyptian government ensured that everything remained in its homeland. Carter and Carnarvon, however, removed and kept some small items, and those that were still in Carter's possession when he died were discreetly returned to Egypt. The reality of the tomb's discovery and clearance was much messier and more complex than many official accounts suggest, and the day-by-day records in the archive tell 'a chronicle no longer gold',[7] but one that is arguably more revealing. The archive also enables a more inclusive view of the team and its work.

Figure 4 A view of the tomb and its contents as imagined in a measured perspective drawing by Harold Parkinson (1918–1995), based on photographs from the archive, 1978. H. Parkinson MSS 1.

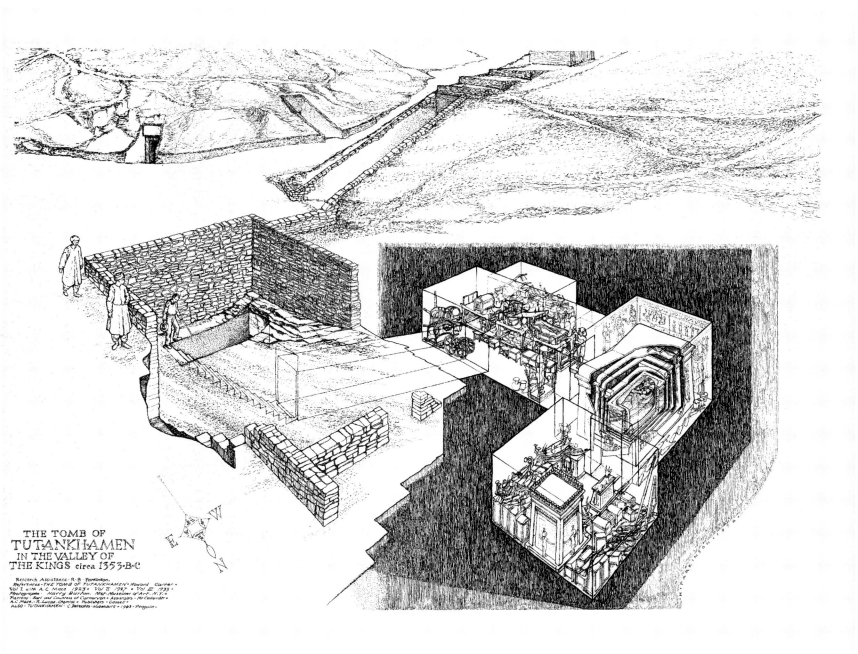

THE TOMB OF
TUTANKHAMEN
IN THE VALLEY OF
THE KINGS circa 1353·B·C

Research Assistance· R·B· Parkinson·
References·THE TOMB OF TUTANKHAMEN· Howard Carter·
Vol I with A.C Mace · 1923· Vol II · 1987 · Vol III · 1933·
Photographs· Harry Burton· Met Museum of Art· N.Y.·
Patrons· Earl and Countess of Carnarvon· Assistants· Mr Callender·
A.C Mace· R. Lucas Chemist · Publishers · Cassell·
ALSO· TUTANKHAMEN· C Desroches-Noblecourt · 1963· Penguin·

RECORDING THE TOMB

The scale of the discovery made it a 'tremendous emergency',[8] and an international team was quickly assembled, drawing on an offer of help from the Metropolitan Museum of Art, New York, which had its own archaeological expedition in Luxor and which, of course, hoped to benefit from the expected division of the finds. This loosely gathered team of associates, both professional and personal contacts, included Arthur Mace (1874–1928), an assistant curator at the MMA; Alfred Lucas (1867–1945), a chemist working for the Antiquities Service who conserved the materials; Arthur Callender (1875–1936), an engineer; and Harry Burton (1879–1940), a photographer working for the MMA's Egyptian expedition. All were American or European men, although the Egyptian Dr Saleh Bey Hamdi (d.1957), former director of the Government School of Medicine, Cairo, later conducted the autopsy on the king's mummified body with Douglas Derry (1874–1961), professor of anatomy at the same school. The European depression encouraged the discovery to be reported to the world as a sensationalist adventure of a type familiar from popular fiction, with all the glamour of gold from an exotic world (Figure 5), but the discovery was not simply an adventure by heroic men, despite the way in which many people, including Carter himself, have presented it. Workers on the project included a few women such as Harry Burton's wife Minnie (1875–1957). Above all, Egyptians were central to the discovery, including the chief foreman (*rais*) Ahmed Gerigar, and his colleagues Gad Hassan, Hussein Abu Awad and Hussein Ahmed Said (dates unrecorded).[9] These Egyptian members of the excavation were named and thanked in Carter's publications, but Egyptians were otherwise (and in general) rarely named in the records, and their role was downplayed in official accounts; nevertheless, their crucial presence is made visible by the archive's photographs which reveal their contribution (Figure 6).

The clearance of the tomb was such a long and difficult process owing to the quantity, variety and fragility of the artefacts, which included not only

CHURCHMAN'S CIGARETTES

THE TOMB OF TUT-ANKH-AMEN : THE FIRST INSPECTION

Figure 5 A public sensation: a cigarette card showing the English entering the tomb in November 1922, based on an illustration by Amédée Forestier (1854–1930) for *The Illustrated London News*, 22 December 1923. TAA iii.25.1.26.

Figure 6 Photograph by *The Times* showing Carter and an Egyptian team member carrying part of a ritual bed (Carter no. 137) up the stairs together, February 1923. The person shown taking a photograph (bottom right) is probably Lord Carnarvon; a padded container lies ready to transport the object to the conservation laboratory. TAA ii.19.70.4.

gold and semi-precious stones, but also painted wood, cloth, perfumed oils, animal and human remains, bread, fruit and even flowers. The complex assemblages were material embodiments of ancient processes of grief and mourning. Photography was used to record the tomb, and Burton produced some of 'the most famous and compelling archaeological images ever made'.[10] During the clearance, photographs were first taken of an area of the tomb, and then again when numbered cards had been placed beside each object. Individual objects and groups of objects were numbered in a sequence 1–620 with subdivisions, totalling over 5,300 separate items. Once the objects were removed from their findspot, they were recorded on index cards with dimensions and drawings, conserved and photographed again. There was an attempt to be as systematic and scientific as possible, despite the physical constraints of the desert site. Burton developed his glass plate negatives in a nearby tomb, repurposed as a studio, and it is estimated that he took well over 3,000 shots in these difficult conditions. Inevitably, the records were not always as thorough as intended, and during the archaeological clearance the objects became removed and isolated from their complex context, but the archive records and preserves this (unavoidably) lost context and documents the process of clearing.

Soon after the discovery, on 9 January 1923, Carnarvon signed a deal granting exclusive rights to *The Times* newspaper, hoping to regain some of the costs of the work, and so Burton's images include many carefully staged photographs designed specifically for publication and publicity, as well as less formal shots of the team at work (Figure 7). The controversial deal alienated many, including most importantly the Egyptian press, and there were complaints that Carnarvon was 'exploiting' the find and treating it as a personal 'commercial asset'.[11] When Carnarvon died after a short illness on 5 April 1923, a hostile press indulged in sensational tales of his having been struck down by an ancient curse. For Egyptians, however, Tutankhamun was becoming 'an icon of national independence'.[12] After the Egyptian Egyptologist Selim Hassan (1886–1961) visited the tomb, he wrote that 'for the first time, the Egyptian people proclaimed that these precious antiquities should remain in the Egyptian Museum'.[13] During the course of the tomb's clearance, laws and policies changed and, thanks to the Egyptian government, the Egyptian Museum in Tahrir Square in Cairo was the objects' permanent home until the inauguration of the new displays in the Grand Egyptian Museum at Giza.

Figure 7 An apparently informal photograph (slightly blurred) by Harry Burton of Carter at work in the tomb, sitting in the entrance to the Burial chamber, between 10 and 12 February 1924. Behind him are the panels of the gilded shrines. Burton P0636.

THE ARCHIVE IN OXFORD

The study of the entire tomb, and the preparation of a comprehensive publication, were a burden for Carter that he was incapable of fulfilling. While he completed a best-selling preliminary three-volume account in 1933, he had not made much progress on a planned six-volume academic publication before he died in 1939, aged sixty-five. The excavation had not been conducted by the Egyptian authorities but on a concession granted by them to Lord Carnarvon and his heirs; Carter as his excavator and agent was in charge of recording and publishing the work, and as such he retained the ownership of his team's records.[14] Carter bequeathed most of his estate to his favourite niece, Phyllis Walker (1897–1977) (Figure 8), who had spent a season in 1931 with him in Luxor. His estate included the archaeological records stored in his flat in London, and following the advice of the Egyptologists Alan H. Gardiner (1879–1963) and Percy E. Newberry (1869–1949), who had both been on the team, she donated the documentation with associated copyright to the Griffith Institute, the centre for Egyptology at the University

Figure 8 Phyllis Walker as a child in a family photograph, around 1903. Carter MSS viii.3.

of Oxford, 'as a memorial to him and his work'.[15] Many of these records had already been sent as a protective deposit to Oxford on 26 August 1939, away from the dangers of London as war loomed, and in early 1946 Carter's set of Burton's negatives and prints joined them from storage in London. A second set of these images (though not an exact duplicate) had earlier been given to the MMA in return for its having lent Burton's services to Carter.

The Tutankhamun archive in Oxford comprises some forty-eight maps and plans, seven card index drawers with over 3,500 object cards with associated photographic prints, around 1,200 original glass negatives and over 600 lantern slides, as well as sets of duplicate negatives and photographs. The archive also includes Carter's personal diaries and archaeological journals, notes and drawings for the planned publication, Lucas's conservation logbooks and notes, records of the unwrapping and examination of the king's body, as well as Carter's draft 'Autobiographical Sketches' and earlier documentation for his excavations at other sites. At the start of the 1950s, the Oxford archive and the MMA made an exchange of images to fill gaps in both sets of the Burton photographs. The Oxford archive continues to acquire new relevant material, expanding and diversifying the original holdings, and the collection is stored in the Egyptological archive of the Griffith Institute, preserving in part its original arrangement by Carter.

Although the physical archive remains in Oxford as part of the processes that created it, it is shared internationally in the digital world. From the 1990s onwards, the records were published online by the then keeper of the archive, the Egyptologist Jaromir Malek, as *Tutankhamun: Anatomy of an Excavation* (www.griffith.ox.ac.uk/discoveringTut). The archive is a rich and accessible resource for research (Figure 9), allowing scholars continually to reassess the burial and its discovery. As one minor example, Carter's famous words on first looking into the tomb were recorded in his publication of 1923 as 'wonderful things', but his Excavation journal gives them as 'it is wonderful', suggesting that this – perhaps the most famous line in the history of archaeology – was a later elaboration.[16] Most importantly of all, however, the archive is always accessible to assist the curation, conservation, publication and display of the objects in Cairo.

STORIES AND RECEPTION

Stories gathered quickly around the discovery of the tomb, such as the supposed curse on an imaginary ancient tablet that led to Carnarvon's death, and Carter's own anecdote that the steps of the entrance were first found by

a young Egyptian water carrier.[17] Such reshapings of events were generated by persons and institutions with vested interests: the history of Egyptology as a whole is deeply embedded in, and irrevocably shaped by, colonialism. The archive is itself inevitably a highly partial view of the events, created by people who were complicit in this world and its power structures. In the 1920s, Egypt was changing under the leadership of Saad Zaghloul (1859–1927), and its pharaonic past was helping to shape a new sense of national identity. The limited role of Egyptians and the lack of Egyptian voices in the Carter archive starkly reveal the inequalities of power in both social and academic worlds. Burton's photographs have often been used in exhibitions in ways that uncritically endorse a nostalgic story of a golden age of archaeology, 'vintage' colonialism. The popular appeal of the 'treasures' of Tutankhamun has unwittingly added to the legacy of orientalism and colonialism: this aftermath is perhaps the real 'curse' to emerge from the tomb. For decades after the original 'Tutmania' craze of the 1920s, multiple appropriations have seen Tutankhamun used to sell commodities, to legitimize histories of nations and academic disciplines, and to generate often misleading and stereotypical views of his ancient world. Nevertheless, the records themselves demand – and repay – constant and renewed interrogation, and that can inspire a critical reassessment of both modern and ancient histories. This capacity is due in part to the fact that, whatever their colonialist contexts and personal limitations, Burton was a fine photographer, and Carter a fine draughtsman with a deep appreciation of ancient artistry. The objects that they recorded have, like any cultural icon, not only given rise to commodification, but also inspired new works of art (Figures 10–11). The tomb and its objects have become integral parts of world heritage.

Nothing can substitute for the sight of the objects themselves in Cairo, but the archival records complement seeing the original artefacts, since they evoke the processes of their deposition in the tomb and their clearance and conservation. With this in mind, we have selected the documents in this book to suggest the complexity both of the burial and of its clearance. The selection shows familiar pieces in unfamiliar ways and settings: statues still wrapped in cloth and world-famous objects piled on top of each other in a cramped clutter. The archive still conveys the visceral emotions of the discovery: the scrawled writing in Carter's diary for 4 November 1922 (no. 5) reveals the excitement felt at finding the steps, in contrast to the hundreds of neatly written pages recording the day-to-day practicalities of his long work. The image of the sawn-off feet of the outer coffin, rectifying an ancient error

Figure 9 A digital colour reconstruction of wall paintings unavoidably destroyed when the partition wall sealing the Burial chamber was taken down, based on Burton photograph P0589. Produced as part of a physical facsimile of the Burial chamber in the Carter House Visitor Centre, Luxor. Factum Foundation 2011.

(no. 27), gives us a 'touch of the real', an immediate sense of ancient lived experience. This alteration to the coffin is instantly recognizable to us as a familiar experience, as well as being utterly different and 'other'. In this way, the archive fosters understanding both of the modern excavation team and of the ancient courtiers, craftsmen and workers who lived these histories. Together, these records and objects can still powerfully engage viewers, decades after the discovery and millennia after the king's funeral, challenging us to re-imagine this past. The Egyptian poet Ahmad Shawqi (1870–1932), who was a friend of Dr Saleh Bey Hamdi, put it best when he wrote about the objects:

Images that show you movement, though their origin is stillness.
The clarity of their silence passes over the senses, like clear speech.
Their paint accompanied time, from ancient age to ancient age.
The paint remains fresh, despite the lengthy trials [of time], and alive, despite the long duration of death.
The paint tricks the eyes and still challenges those who touch it.[18]

Figure 10 A modernist view of the coronation of Tutankhamun as imagined in Philip Glass's opera *Akhnaten*, staged by the Metropolitan Opera New York, with Christian J. Conner as the boy-king. © Karen Almond, Met Opera, 2019.

Figure 11 Modern Egyptian art inspired by a statue of a goddess from the tomb (Carter no. 266): *Selket 2019* by the Luxor-based artist Alaa Awad (b.1981). © Alaa Awad 2019.

FIFTY RECORDS FROM
THE ARCHIVE

I A TEENAGER IN EGYPT

Howard Carter first arrived in Egypt in 1891 at the age of seventeen, as a junior draughtsman for the Egypt Exploration Fund (now Society) based in London, after he had been recommended by a local MP, Baron Amherst of Hackney (1835–1909). A few weeks later, he was working at el-Amarna with the archaeologist William Matthew Flinders Petrie (1853–1942), who occasionally accepted young British men on his excavations to train them in his methods. In this journal-letter of January 1892 (right side), Petrie wrote home to his mother: 'Mr Carter is a good-natured lad, whose interest is entirely in painting & natural history … it is of no use for me to work him up as an excavator'!

Mr Carter came here, & settled in, building a room & roofing it with boards and durra-stalks like mine. His position here is to be as agent for Mr Tyssen Amherst M.P.; he takes much interest in Tell Amarna, & had wished to work here … Hearing of this I offered to allow him to appoint a worker to dig for him under my permission, provided I controlled the work & had the exhibiting & publishing of what was found. Thus I expand the amount of ground worked & the information, without any responsibility or expense to myself … Mr Carter is a good-natured lad, whose interest is entirely in painting & natural history; he only takes this digging as being on the spot & convenient to Mr Amherst, & it is of no use for me to work him up as an excavator.

The main matter this week has been turning over some remains of amulet factories …

At the painted pavements the second room is now finished; & the posts & roofing & windows are next required. After it is all done, I shall have a long job ?? after cleaning out the inside, fixing the colours, fitting gangways, &c. Very possibly I shall stay on in Ramadan (April) drawing the floors, as I could do that comfortably during the heat in those large rooms, & have no work going on outside. I have asked Pickard if he could join me for a fortnight in Sicily on my way home, in April or May.

Many pieces of cartouches of Khuenaten, of Nefertiti, & of the Aten are continually being turned up; & I have a stack of about a couple of tons of stone lying in my courtyard, which is mostly worth carrying away, although fragmentary.

Mrs Petrie, 8. Crescent R.
Bromley, Kent.

3–9 Jan 1892   Mr. Carter came here, & settles in, building a room & roofing it with boards & durra-stalks like mine. His position here is to be as agent for Mr. Tyssen Amherst M.P.; she takes much interest in Tell Amarna, & had wished to work here. Hearing of this, I offered to him to allow him to appoint a worker to dig for him under my permission, provided I controlled the work & had the exhibiting & publishing of what was found. Thus I expand the amount of ground worked & the information, without any responsibility or expence to myself. I was also hoping to have expanded my own work by Mr. Blackden coming to join me personally; but his engagements to the committee tied him so that he could not arrange it. Mr. Carter is a good-natured lad, whose interest is entirely in painting & natural history; he only takes this digging ?? as being on the spot & convenient to Mr. Amherst, & it is of no use for me to work him up as an excavator. The main matter this week has been turning over some remains of amulet factories; over a thousand pottery moulds have been found,

2 THE YOUNG ARTIST

Carter's draughtsmanship ensured his success in Egypt. He was born into
a family of artists, and he later recalled: 'we all inherited from our father an
inborn faculty for drawing: he being an animal painter of no little fame,
and one of the most powerful draughtsmen I ever knew.' By the mid-1890s
Carter was recording wall scenes in the temple of Hatshepsut at Luxor for the
Egypt Exploration Fund, and sometimes in colour. This '3/4 full size' copy
of a painted relief 'from Hypostyle Hall' depicting a falcon shows Carter's
engagement with ancient Egyptian art and interest in wildlife. He detailed
the blocks of the wall and the damage to their surface, adding his own
flamboyant signature.

**Horus falcon, the hall of the chapel
of Anubis, temple of Hatshepsut,
Deir el-Bahari**
Watercolour on paper, 63.9 × 97.7 cm
Howard Carter, 1895
Griffith Institute Watercolours and
Drawings 204

Howard Carter. — 1895 —
from Hypostyle Hall. — 3/4 Full Size.

(15)

3 'LORD C.'

This photograph shows Lord Carnarvon as a leisured and aristocratic amateur archaeologist, relaxing with a book in Carter's house on the west bank at Luxor, perhaps while he was staying there to be close to the Valley of the Kings. Like many items in the archive, this is undated, and although the half-plate negative is a different size from those usually used by Harry Burton (see no. 15), the style and composition suggest that it was taken by him during the first excavation season in 1922–3. With hindsight, the restful pose is ominous: Carnarvon's health was poor, and on 5 April 1923 he died of sepsis from an infected mosquito bite.

George Edward Stanhope Molyneux Herbert, 5th earl of Carnarvon
Glass plate negative, 12 × 16.3 cm
Probably Harry Burton, perhaps early 1923
Burton KV93

4 A MAP OF FIVE YEARS' WORK

This map charts Carnarvon's archaeological concession in the eastern part of the Valley of the Kings at Luxor. Carter drew and updated it during their excavations between 1917 and 1922. Over a pencilled grid of referenced squares, he plotted known royal tombs and other features, indicating landmarks in yellow, and he updated it as he methodically worked along the valley floor, excavating down to the bedrock. He later claimed that, when Carnarvon's commitment to the excavations had faltered, he used this map to argue for one more season in 1922 to clear the last area (lower centre). Tellingly, the map was not updated after the start of this season on 1 November 1922.

Map of the Valley of the Kings
Ink, pencil and watercolour on paper,
65.9 × 99.6 cm
Howard Carter, between 1917 and 1922
Carter MSS i.G.51
also shown on following pages

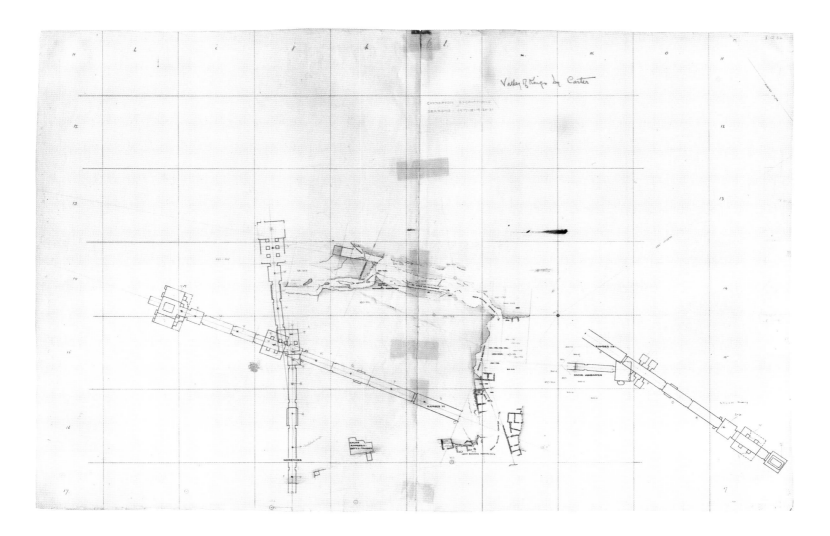

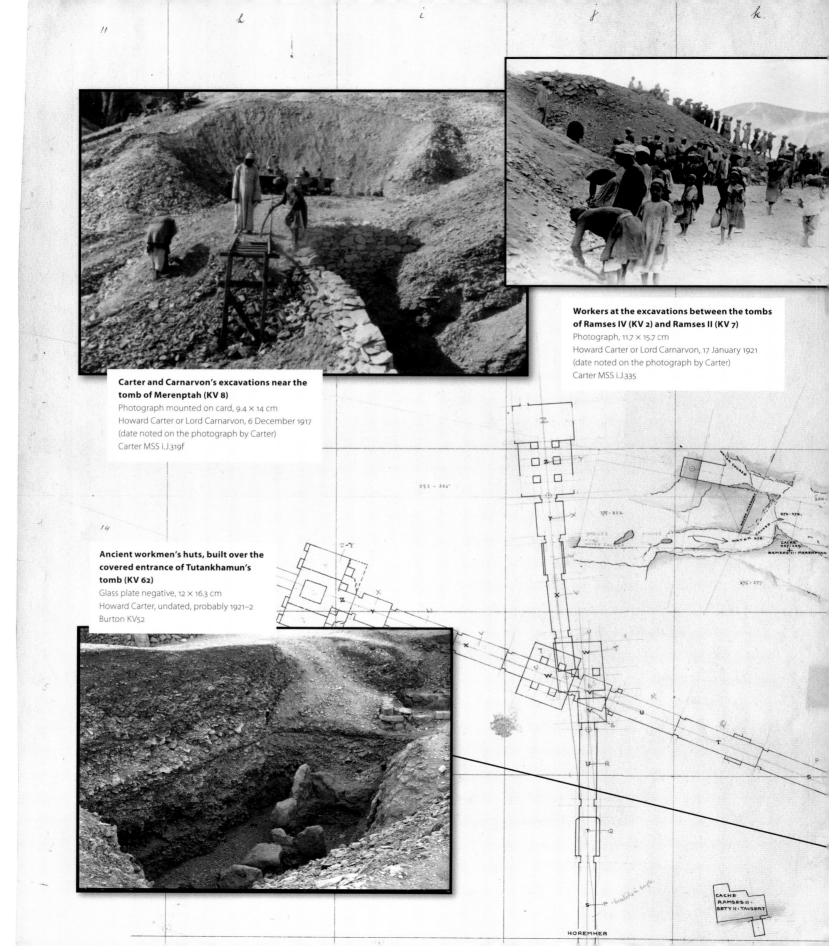

Carter and Carnarvon's excavations near the tomb of Merenptah (KV 8)
Photograph mounted on card, 9.4 × 14 cm
Howard Carter or Lord Carnarvon, 6 December 1917
(date noted on the photograph by Carter)
Carter MSS i.J.319f

Workers at the excavations between the tombs of Ramses IV (KV 2) and Ramses II (KV 7)
Photograph, 11.7 × 15.7 cm
Howard Carter or Lord Carnarvon, 17 January 1921
(date noted on the photograph by Carter)
Carter MSS i.J.335

Ancient workmen's huts, built over the covered entrance of Tutankhamun's tomb (KV 62)
Glass plate negative, 12 × 16.3 cm
Howard Carter, undated, probably 1921–2
Burton KV52

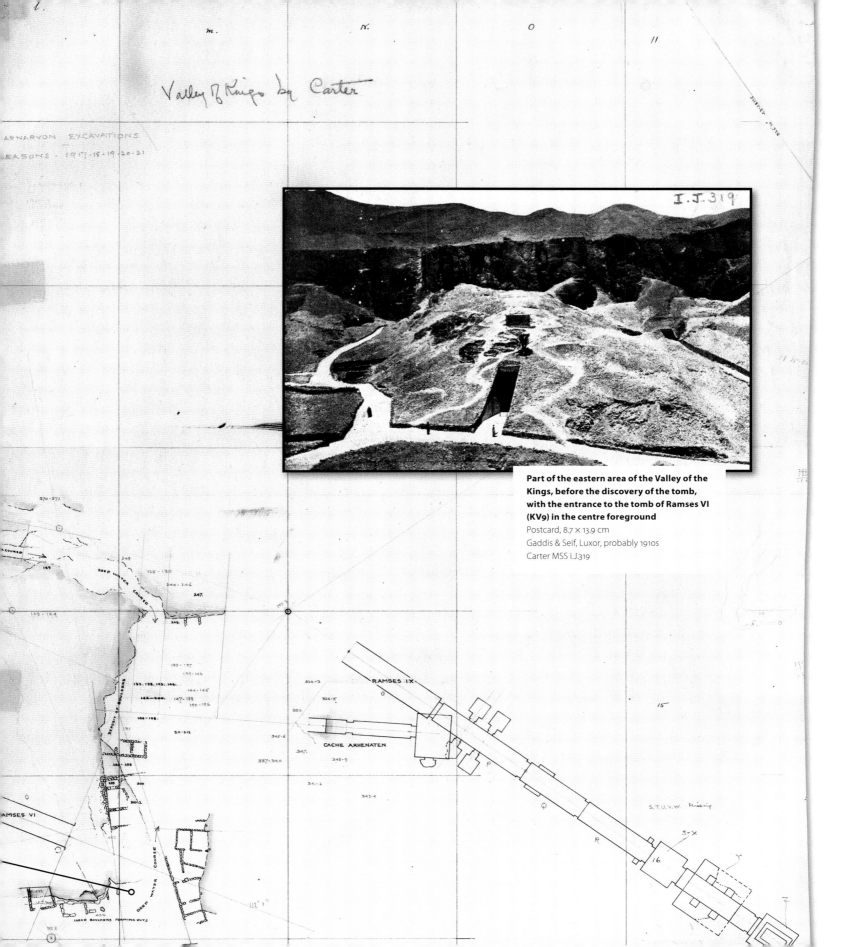

I.J.319

Valley of Kings by Carter

CARNARVON EXCAVATIONS
SEASONS · 1917·18·19·20·21

Part of the eastern area of the Valley of the Kings, before the discovery of the tomb, with the entrance to the tomb of Ramses VI (KV9) in the centre foreground
Postcard, 8.7 × 13.9 cm
Gaddis & Seif, Luxor, probably 1910s
Carter MSS i.J.319

RAMSES IX

CACHE AKHENATEN

RAMSES VI

5 'FOUND'

Carter used a pocket-size Letts's 'Indian and Colonial Rough Diary' to record his activities in the eight months that he worked in Egypt each year. Neat, concise entries noted his departures and arrivals, lunch appointments, meetings with officials and colleagues, and his excavations. In 1922 he and his team started work in the Valley of the Kings on 1 November, and three days later he scribbled a single line in pencil across the page, a graphic sign of his excitement as he recorded 'First steps of tomb found'. The next day he wrote more evenly, 'Discovered tomb under tomb of Ramses VI[.] Investigated same & found seals intact' – a fact suggesting that this was the entrance to an undisturbed royal tomb.

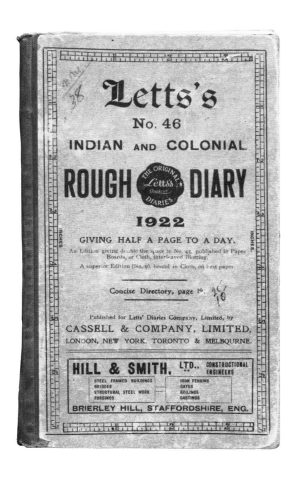

Letts's Rough Diary for 1922
Paper, board and cloth; pencil and ink,
19.7 × 12 × 1.7 cm (closed)
Howard Carter, 4 November 1922
TAA Archive i.2.21.175–6

2 THURSDAY [306—59]

4 SATURDAY [308—57]

3 FRIDAY [307—58]

6 THE FIRST STEP

This is one of the very first photographs of Tutankhamun's tomb. All of the rock-cut steps of the entrance are covered with limestone chips, apart from the topmost one. Carter cleared these steps on 5 November, but then re-covered them until Carnarvon could travel to Luxor from England to witness the discovery. This view, which shows Carter's backfill and the newly built retaining wall, was taken before the team started to uncover the steps again on 23 November, as soon as Carnarvon arrived. Carter and Carnarvon quickly recognized the limits of their photographic expertise, and in early December requested the services of Harry Burton from the Metropolitan Museum's expedition at Luxor.

Entrance to the tomb of Tutankhamun (KV 62);
width of steps: 160 cm
Glass plate negative, 10.7 × 8.2 cm
Howard Carter or Lord Carnarvon, probably
23 November 1922
Burton P0001

7 'IT IS WONDERFUL'

As well as his diary, Carter kept an Excavation journal. Around 4 p.m. on 26 November, accompanied by Egyptian workmen, Callender, Carnarvon and Lady Evelyn Herbert (Carnarvon's daughter), Carter made a hole through the inner doorway of the tomb and looked inside for the first time. This journal entry describes the suspense of the 'Great Moment' in a self-consciously vivid style. In his later publication, however, he described it differently: 'when Lord Carnarvon … inquired anxiously, "Can you see anything?" it was all I could do to get out the words, "Yes, wonderful things".' The phrase 'it is wonderful' in the more contemporaneous journal is probably closer to the actual phrase spoken.

opposite **Excavation journal for 26 November 1922**
Ink on squared paper, 33.1 × 21.7 cm
Howard Carter, some time after 26 November 1922
TAA Archive i.2.1.35

below **Carter's writing desk-set from his house at Luxor**
Silver and glass, 5.2 × 21.8 × 14 cm (max.)
Henry and Arthur Vander of London, 1912
Carter MSS viii.1

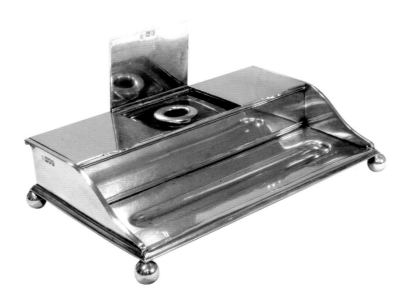

It was sometime before one could see, the hot air escaping caused the candle to flicker, but as soon as one's eyes became accustomed to the glimmer of light the interior of the chamber gradually loomed before one, with its strange and wonderful medley of extraordinary and beautiful objects heaped upon one another. There was naturally short suspence [sic] for those present who could not see, when Lord Carnarvon said to me 'Can you see anything'. I replied to him [']Yes, it is wonderful[']. I then with precaution made the hole sufficiently large for both of us to see. With the light of an electric torch as well as an additional candle we looked in. Our sensations and astonishment are difficult to describe as the better light revealed to us the marvellous collection of treasures: two strange ebony-black effigies of a King, gold sandalled [sic], bearing staff and mace, loomed out from the cloak of darkness … stools of all shapes and design, of both common and rare materials; and, lastly a confusion of overturned parts of chariots glinting with gold, peering from amongst which was a mannikin. The first impression of which suggested the property-room of an opera-house of a vanished civilization. Our sensations were bewildering and full of strange emotion. We questioned one another as to the meaning of it all. Was it a tomb or merely a cache?

(Nov. 26 Continued)

It was sometime before one could see, the hot air escaping caused the candle to flicker, but as soon as one's eyes became accustomed to the glimmer of light, the interior of the chamber gradually loomed before one, with its strange and wonderful medley of extraordinary and beautiful objects heaped upon one another. There was naturally short suspense for those present who could not see, when Lord Carnarvon said to me "Can you see anything?" I replied to him Yes, it is wonderful. I then with precaution made the hole sufficiently large for both of us to see. With the light of an electric torch as well as an additional candle we looked in. Our sensations and astonishment are difficult to describe as the better light revealed to us the marvellous collection of treasures: two strange ebony-black effigies of a King, gold sandalled, bearing staff and mace, loomed out from the cloak of darkness; gilded couches in strange forms, lion-headed, Hathor-headed, and beast infernal; exquisitely painted, inlaid, and ornamental caskets; flowers; alabaster vases, some beautifully executed of lotus and papyrus device; strange black shrines with a gilded monster appearing from within; quite ordinary looking white chests; finely carved chairs; a golden inlaid throne; a heap of large curious white oviform boxes; beneath our very eyes, on the threshold, a lovely lotiform wishing-cup in translucent alabaster; stools of all shapes and design, of both common and rare materials; and, lastly a confusion of over turned chariots glinting with gold, peering from amongst which was a magnificent furniture of a vanished civilization. The first impression of which suggested the property-room of an Opera. Our sensations were bewildering and full of strange emotion. We questioned one another as to the meaning of it all. Was it a tomb or merely a cache? A sealed doorway between the two sentinel statues proved there was more beyond, and with the numerous cartouches bearing the name of Tut-Ankh-Amen on most of the objects before us, there was little doubt that there behind was the grave of that Pharoah.

We closed the hole, locked the wooden-grill which had been placed upon the first doorway, we mounted our donkeys and return home contemplating what we had seen.

Advised the Chief Inspector of the Antiquity Department, who was with us at the commencement of the opening of the first doorway, and asked him to come as soon as possible, preferably the following afternoon to enable us to prepare an electrical installation for careful inspection of this extraordinary and pleasing discovery.

8 A VIEW INTO THE TOMB

This photograph by Burton shows the view that Carter saw when he first looked into the tomb on 26 November. The photograph was taken quite some time later, after electric lights had been installed and after Burton had started work on 18 December. Nevertheless, this famous image recaptures the sight that Carter evoked in the Excavation journal: 'gilded couches in strange forms, lion-headed, Hathor-headed, and beast infernal; exquisitely painted, inlaid, and ornamental caskets' (see no. 7). Around the ritual beds, stools (including no. 42) and storage boxes are stacked up, including 'a heap of large curious white oviform boxes' containing joints of meat.

View of the west side of the Antechamber with objects; height of ritual bed (Carter no. 73): 188 cm (max.)
Glass plate negative, 17.9 × 23.9 cm
Harry Burton, shortly after 18 December 1922
Burton P0009

9 'THE GREATEST FIND EVER'

Scrawled on both sides of this single sheet is Carnarvon's vivid account of the discovery. On 28 November 1922, just before the tomb was officially opened, he wrote to the Egyptologist Alan Gardiner to give an account of what they had seen. His rapidly written, almost incoherent words convey the shock of their first sight of the 'marvellous' objects (see nos 7, 8). Carnarvon was immediately aware of the scale of the discovery, although not of the full implications this would have for everyone: it would take much more than 'weeks of work' to conserve and clear the 'packed' tomb.

Most private
My dear Gardiner
I wrote to my wife yesterday & asked her to give you a message.
The find is extraordinary it is a cache & has been plundered to a certain extent but even the ancients could not completely destroy it after some slight plundering the [ancient] inspectors shut it again. So far it is Tutankamon beds boxes & every conceivable thing there is a box with a few papyri in [actually rolls of linen] – the throne of the King the most marvellous inlaid chair you ever saw – 2 life size figures of the King bitumenised [sic] – all sorts of religious signs hardly known up to date[]
The King['s] clothing rotten but gorgeous. Everything is in a very ticklish state owing to constant handlings & openings in ancient times (I reckon on having to spend 2000£ on preserving & packing)[] …
Then there is a bricked up room which we have not yet opened[] Probably containing the mummies …
There is enough stuff to fill the whole Egyptian section upstairs of the B.M. I imagine it is the greatest find ever made. Tomorrow the official opening & before I leave we peep into the walled chamber … I hope to be back soon. Carter has weeks of work ahead of him[] I have between 20 & 30 soldiers police & gaffirs [watchmen] to guard.
Yours C.

Letter from Lord Carnarvon to Alan Gardiner
Ink on paper, 25.2 × 20.1 cm (page); 11.2 × 14.5 cm
(envelope)
Lord Carnarvon, 28 November 1922 (undated)
Gardiner MSS, Newspaper Cuttings Album, 1.39.1 (recto
and verso)

Most private

My dear Gardiner

I wrote to my wife yesterday & asked her to give you
a message.

The find is extraordinary ~~stuff~~ It is a cache & has been
plundered to a certain extent but even the ancients could
not completely destroy it. After some slight plundering the
inspectors shut it again. So far it is Tutankamon
~~and~~ beds boxes & every conceivable thing there is
a box with a few papyri in – the throne of the King the
most marvellous inlaid chair you ever saw –

2 life size figures of the King bitumenised all sorts of
religious signs hardly known up to date The King clothing
rotten but gorgeous. Everything is in a very ticklish state owing
to constant handlings & openings in ancient times
(I reckon on having to spend 2000£ on preserving &
packing) The most wonderful ushabti in wood of the
King wood portrait head ditto endless staves etc

Tone with most wonderful work 4 chariots

The most miraculous alabaster vases ever seen

3 colossal beds of honour with extraordinary animals
There is a further room so packed one cant see really
what is there – ~~Some~~ of the boxes are marvellous
chairs innumerable a wonderful stool ~~X~~ ebony
& ivory

Then there is a bricked up room which we have
not yet opened Probably containing the mummies
I should not be surprised to find therein
Tut & his wife & Smenkkara & his, but so far
its all Tut.

There is enough stuff to fill the whole Egyptian
section upstairs of the B.M.
I imagine it is the greatest find ever made.
To morrow the official opening
& before I leave we peep into the walled
Chamber.

I some how fancy it is the whole of the Amarna
outfit as on the throne the King & wife are represented
with sun disk. I work
I hope to be back soon. Carter has weeks ahead of
him I have between 20 x 30 soldiers police
& Gaffirs to guard –

IO   SURVEYING THE TOMB

This is the most detailed scaled plan of the tomb produced during the excavation. Drawn up by Carter, it represents the small tomb in its original state, including the sealed doorways and the partition wall that closed off the Burial chamber. Carter tried to record every detail, adding measurements and annotations. His working notes in faint pencil include additions and calculations, with the sweeping lines of a compass used to plot the rooms. He indicated the chipped treads of the stairs and marked a natural fissure in the limestone running diagonally across the ceiling of the Antechamber and Burial chamber.

Captions identify the rooms with the names that Carter gave them:

ANTECHAMBER

ANNEXE (A STOREROOM)

BURIAL CHAMBER

INNERMOST TREASURY

By the doorway and steps is written:

Reveals cut away a

Lintel cut away b

Six Steps cut away c

a, b, c afterwards made good with plaster[.]

They were cut away to enable larger objects to pass in Tomb.

Annotated plan of tomb, 1:40; north is to the right
Pencil on paper, 54.3 × 56.3 cm
Howard Carter, dated 'Dec. 1923' (before the Burial chamber was officially opened), but completed no earlier than 1930
Carter MSS i.G.4

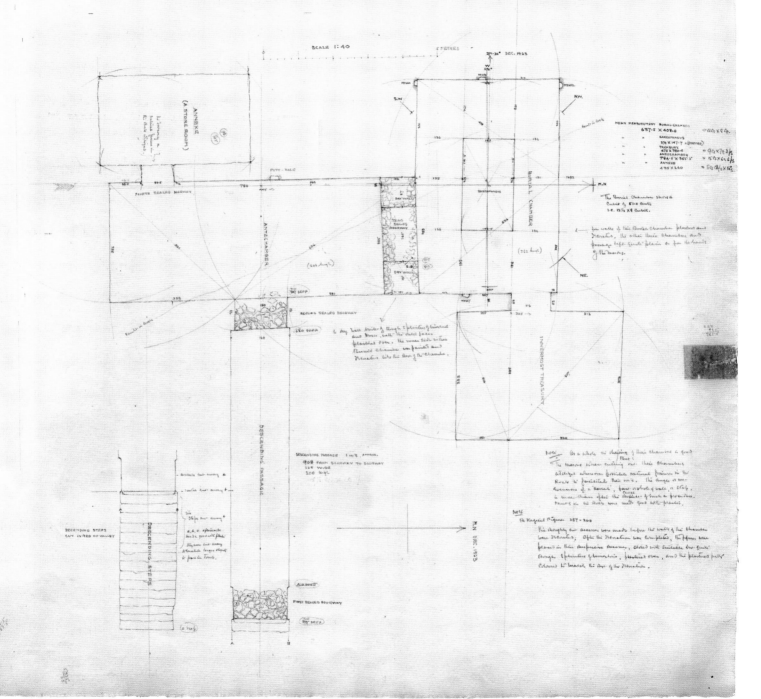

SCALE 1:40   5 METRES   271·30° DEC. 1923

I.G.4.

ANNEXE
(A STORE ROOM)

BURIAL CHAMBER

SARCOPHAGUS

ANTECHAMBER

INNERMOST TREASURY

DESCENDING PASSAGE

DESCENDING STEPS
CUT IN RED OF VALLEY

DESCENDING STEPS

M.N. DEC. 1923

FIRST SEALED DOORWAY

II 'LUNCH NEAR THE TOMB'

As soon as Carter and Carnarvon realized the extent of the discovery, they gathered a team of experts together. This photograph was apparently taken by Carnarvon, and shows the group seated for lunch in Ramses XI's rock-cut tomb, near Tutankhamun's. The lunchers – all English-speaking and all white men – are (left to right): James Henry Breasted (1865–1935, to work on the door seals), Burton, Lucas (conservation), Callender (engineering), Mace (object recording and conservation), Carter and Gardiner (texts). Carnarvon's own chair at the head of the table is unoccupied; the gentlemen are waited on by unidentified Egyptian servants.

Lunch in the tomb of Ramses XI (KV 4)
Glass plate negative made from original print, 11.9 × 16.3 cm, donated by Alan Gardiner
Lord Carnarvon, probably mid-February 1923
Burton P1544

LUNCH NEAR THE TOMB OF TUTANKHAMUN

CALLENDER   MACE

12 THE UNNAMED TEAM

One day in early December 1923, three Egyptian team members paused in the middle of work for Burton's camera, lit by a strong electric light. This is one of several photographs showing the same group of two foremen and a boy (here holding a basket to remove rubble) in the process of carefully dismantling a partition wall and opening up the Burial chamber. Carter depended on a group of skilled and experienced Egyptians who had worked alongside him for many years, and who were able to meet all the challenges and practical difficulties of the discovery. The names of these members of the team, who included children, were usually not mentioned, but archival research is enabling the role of Egyptians in early excavations to be recognized, redressing this wrong.

Removal of the wall between the Antechamber and the Burial chamber
Glass plate negative, 23.9 × 17.9 cm
Harry Burton, probably 1 or 2 December 1923
Burton P0504

13 PLANNING THE ANTECHAMBER

This scaled plan records the position of the objects on the floor of the first room, known as the Antechamber (see no. 10). It was drawn by two members of the Metropolitan Museum's expedition team in Luxor, Lindsley Foote Hall (1883–1969) and Walter Hauser (1893–1959). The pair conveyed the multilayered arrangement of the objects with pencils and coloured inks, using red to highlight overlapping items, including the king's chairs and stools, as well as parts of four dismantled chariots (lower left corner). Meticulous draughtsmanship allows the viewer to distinguish the various items, each labelled with its object number (see no. 14).

Plan of the Antechamber, 1:10, with objects in place; north is to the right
Black and red ink and pencil on tracing paper, 52.5 × 85.8 cm
Lindsley Foote Hall and Walter Hauser, probably between late December 1922 and 25 April 1923
Carter MSS i.G.11

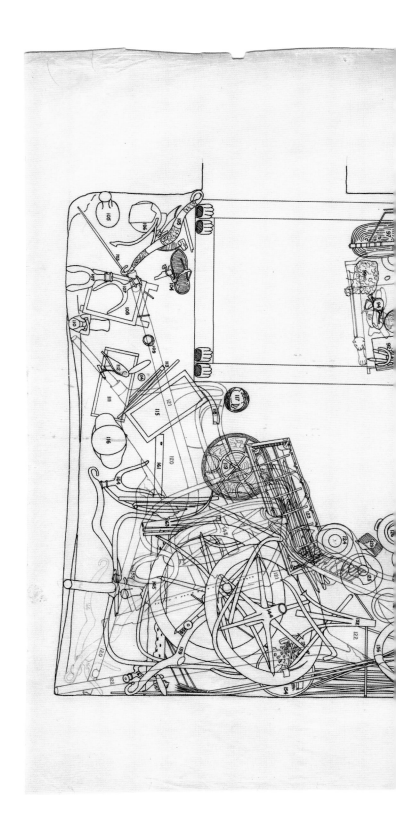

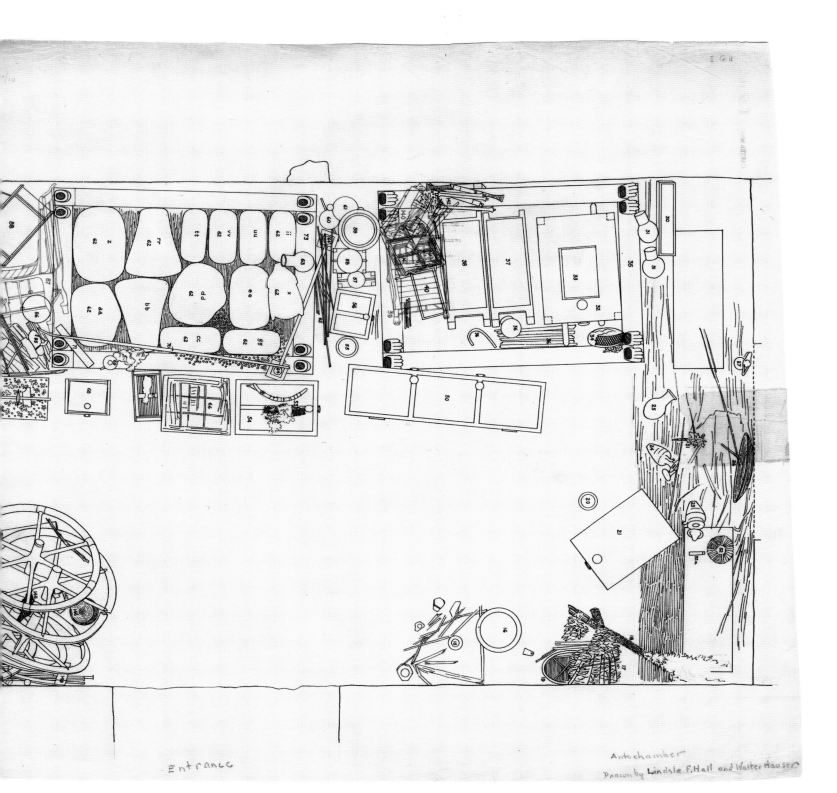

Entrance

Antechamber

Drawn by Lindsle F. Hall and Walter Hauser

14 THE NUMBERING SYSTEM

For his photographic record of the tomb, Burton took two views of each area, one showing all the objects in place, and another after numbered cards (measuring around 5 × 10 cm) had been placed beside each object, assigning it a reference number. This photograph records a corner of the Antechamber, with calcite vessels (Carter nos 16, 20), fragile funerary floral bouquets (nos 17–19) and a richly painted box (no. 21). The photograph, however, may be deceptive: some modern scholars have suggested that Carter had previously moved the box and some other objects in order to conceal a hole in the sealed doorway in the partition wall (visible on the left) that he had made to investigate the Burial chamber unofficially.

View of the north-east corner of the Antechamber with numbered objects; height of large vessel (Carter no. 16): 34.5 cm
Glass plate negative, 17.9 × 23.9 cm
Harry Burton, between 18 and
27 December 1922
Burton P0016

15 GLASS PLATE NEGATIVES

Most of Burton's photographs were taken on glass plate negatives coated with a silver and gelatine emulsion. The heavy and fragile unexposed plate was first unwrapped in darkness, placed in a lightfast holder with a sliding panel and then fitted into the back of the camera. To capture an image, Burton focused the camera, inserted a plate holder and removed the panel. The exposures were carefully calculated and often took several seconds or even minutes. A nearby tomb was used as a darkroom for chemically processing each plate. The resulting negatives are so large and fine that they surpass the detail of high-resolution digital photographs.

above **Harry Burton with his camera, at work outside the conservation laboratory in the tomb of Sety II (KV 15)**
35 mm contact print, 3.2 × 1.9 cm
Unknown photographer for *The Times*, probably February 1923
TAA Archive ii.19.14.1.3

opposite **Negative with storage canisters**
Glass plate negative, with a view of the Antechamber (see no. 39), 17.9 × 23.9 cm
Two tinplate negative canisters, labelled 'Sensitive to Light! To be opened only in the presence of the receiver', (a) 25.6 × 19.6 × 11.3 cm; (b) 25.8 × 19.6 × 9.1 cm
Harry Burton, between 18 and 27 December 1922 (negative); 1920s to early 1930s (canisters)
Burton negative P0012; (a) TAA Archive ii.25.1; (b) TAA Archive ii.25.2

16 RECORDING ONE OBJECT

Under one of the ritual beds in the Antechamber, there was a golden throne (Carter no. 91) made early in the king's reign and showing signs of having been used often, possibly at banquets. Burton photographed the throne in position with its number card on the seat, and then took thirteen photos from different angles, including one showing the ancient bands of linen used to transport it. Ten records cards, written by the various team members, provided primary information: Carter's description of the object and its location, his annotated drawing on squared paper and a heavily annotated photograph recording colours and materials, Gardiner's copies of the inscriptions and Lucas's notes on conservation.

left and below **Object cards documenting Tutankhamun's throne (Carter no. 91); height of throne: 104 cm**
Cards by Carter and by Lucas (on 'Treatment'), pencil and ink on lined index cards, 12.5 x 20.5 cm
Howard Carter and Alfred Lucas, January to February 1923
Cards: TAA Archive i.1.91.1, 4

opposite **Photographs documenting the throne**
Glass plate negatives, 20.5 x 12.9 cm (left), 15.9 x 11.5 cm (right)
Harry Burton, between 18 and 27 December 1922 (in the tomb), between mid-February and early May 1923
Burton P0032, P0154H

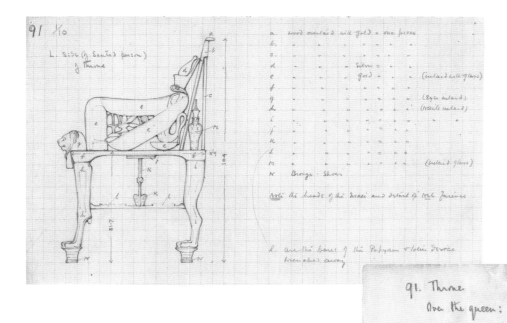

Object cards documenting the throne
Card by Carter, pencil on squared paper, 12.3 x 20.3 cm;
card by Gardiner recording hieroglyphs, blue pencil on
paper, 12.5 x 20.4 cm, photographic print annotated by
Carter with notes on colours and materials, 16.4 x 12.1 cm
Howard Carter and Alan Gardiner, January to
February 1923
TAA Archive i.1.91.5, 8 and annotated print 4

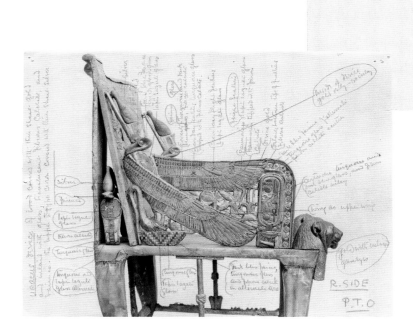

left **Photograph documenting the conserved throne**
Glass plate negative, 17.9 x 11.9 cm
Harry Burton, between mid-February and early May 1923
P0156

below **Colour photograph by John Ross (1920–2006) showing the throne on display in the Egyptian Museum Cairo**
Large format colour positive transparency (quarter plate), 12.5 x 9.9 cm
John Ross, 1960–90s
Ross colour positive 1

17 WRAPPING AND PACKING

In December 1923, at the start of the second season, the team removed the two statues of the king that stood on either side of the entrance to the Burial chamber as if guarding it. This carefully staged tableau shows Carter (left), Callender and an Egyptian team member (right) inside the largely emptied Antechamber, preparing one of the partially gilded statues for transport to the conservation laboratory. The figure has been placed in a custom-made wooden carrying tray, and two of the team hold packing materials. The 'guardian statue' was then ready to leave the tomb, retracing the journey it had made over 3,000 years earlier.

Preparing a 'guardian statue' (Carter no. 22) for transport
Glass plate negative, 17.9 × 23.9 cm
Harry Burton, 29 November 1923
Burton P0491

I8   CLEANING AND CONSERVING

Once an object was removed from the tomb, it was taken to a conservation laboratory set up in the tomb of King Sety II in the Valley of the Kings. There it was documented, cleaned and conserved. This posed photograph shows Arthur Mace (standing on the table) and Alfred Lucas (with a spray) working on one of the 'guardian statues', with their coats and hats hanging on a stand to the left. They dealt with issues such as wood shrinkage and any detaching layers of gilded decoration by applying adhesives and coatings, including celluloid and paraffin wax. Carter commented that without their interventions 'not one-tenth of the many hundreds of objects would ever have reached the Cairo Museum in any reasonable form of condition'.

Conservation of a 'guardian statue' (Carter no. 22) in the tomb of Sety II (KV 15)
Glass plate negative, 23.9 × 17.9 cm
Harry Burton, between 6 and 16 January 1924
Burton P0493

19 A RAILWAY THROUGH THE DESERT

At the end of each season, the conserved objects were boxed and packed in crates. Given the local lack of tarmac roads, a Decauville railway system was used to transport them: short stretches of portable track requiring constant reassembly as the flat-cars were pushed forward. In mid-May 1923, fifty Egyptian workmen spent a total of eighteen hours over two days moving that season's thirty-four crates (containing eighty-nine boxes) the five miles to the river, working in temperatures that reached over 100 °F (38 °C) in the shade. A barge carrying the crates took six days to travel over 400 miles to Cairo, where a selection of the objects were put on immediate display in the Egyptian Museum.

Moving crates from the Valley of the Kings with a Decauville railway system
Glass plate negative, 8.2 × 10.3 cm
Howard Carter, 14 or 15 May 1923
Burton KV16

20 OPENING THE BURIAL CHAMBER

Early in the afternoon of 16 February 1923, about twenty invited guests
– Egyptian dignitaries, Antiquities Service officials and members of the
excavation team – watched tensely in the Antechamber, which was 'as though
set for a stage scene'. Carter and Mace spent two hours opening up the sealed
doorway (labelled as Carter no. 28). On either side the 'guardian statues' were
still in place but protected by wooden covers. Here, Carter (right) pauses as
Carnarvon looks through the opening into the Burial chamber. Once the
opening was big enough, and Carter had made a preliminary inspection,
members of the audience were led in two at a time to view the rooms beyond
– 'each person threw up his hands and gasped'.

   The experience was described by Alan Gardiner in a letter home to his wife
Hedwig in England:

> At last my turn came to be allowed to pass into the new rooms, and with a
> little difficulty I squeezed along … the great heavy door [of] the catafalque
> [outer shrine] had been forced open by Carter, and we could just peep into
> it. Inside was yet another golden shrine of just the same kind, and only
> a little smaller! The inner shrine is sealed and intact … in the tiny space
> between the great and inner golden shrine we could just discern marvellous
> things. Most delightful alabasters, one with a wonderful carved cat upon
> it, and another with a charming Nile-god … in the right hand corner were
> a number of sticks and staves of office, all ornamented with gold.

**Carter opening the Burial chamber's sealed
doorway**
Glass plate negative, 23.9 × 17.9 cm
Harry Burton, 16 February 1923
Burton P0289

2I BEYOND THE WALL

Carter drew this scaled plan after the Burial chamber had been fully investigated; it is a final version traced from earlier working plans. The plan of the tightly packed chamber shows the four shrines of gilded wood, one inside another, which filled almost all the space (as seen on pp. 72–3). It records the position of the various objects placed around and between the nested shrines (everything labelled with its number). At the centre of the shrines is the king's rectangular sarcophagus, shown without its lid and with the top of the gilded outer coffin visible inside (see no. 27). The detailed drawing displays Carter's precision as well as his remarkable artistry.

Plan of the Burial chamber, 1:10, north is at the top
Pencil on tracing paper, 55.6 × 81.2 cm
Howard Carter, completed no earlier than 1930
Carter MSS i.G.31

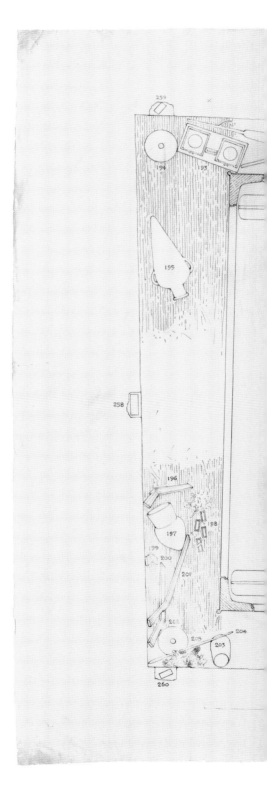

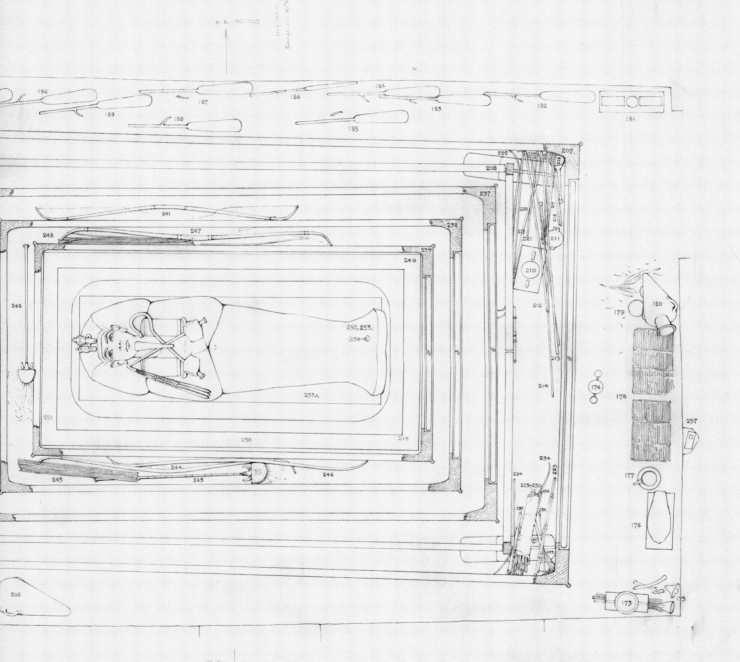

**Photograph through the entrance into
the Burial chamber, almost entirely
filled with the blue and gold outer shrine
(Carter no. 207); height of shrine: 298 cm
(max.)**
Glass plate negative, 17.9 × 23.9 cm
Harry Burton, probably 16 or 17 February 1923
Burton P0603

22 A SCENE FROM THE FUNERAL

The Burial chamber was apparently decorated after the shrines had been erected, and the paint was still fresh when the tomb was sealed; the walls of all the other rooms were left undecorated. This large scene shows 'the courtiers of the palace' dragging the king's mummified body on a sledge in the funerary procession to the tomb. Beneath, a doorway leads into the Treasury, and a small niche in the wall contains a protective statuette, wrapped in linen (Carter no. 257). The chamber was officially entered in 1923, but Burton took this photograph in 1930, after the room had been cleared, and after the sealed niche had been opened during a visit by the Crown Prince of Sweden.

East wall of the Burial chamber; width of doorway: 112 cm
Glass plate negative, 17.9 × 23.9 cm
Harry Burton, probably 3 November 1930 or
shortly afterwards
Burton P0879A

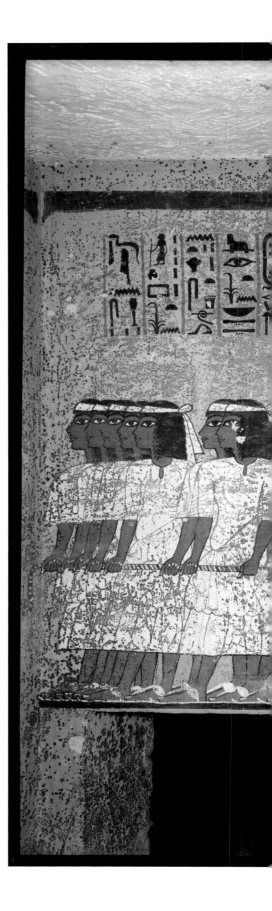

257

23 UNBROKEN SEALS

The great gilded shrines in the Burial chamber were covered with religious scenes and hieroglyphic texts. Inside the first shrine was another, whose doors were still bolted and sealed, showing that everything inside had remained undisturbed since the officials left the tomb in the fourteenth century BCE. Inside that was a third shrine, its doors still fastened shut with a cord neatly tied between two metal loops, and a lump of clay stamped with the official seal of the royal necropolis (a jackal over nine bound enemies). At 3 p.m. on 3 January 1924, Carter 'cut the cords of the seal of the 3rd shrine, [and] opened the folding doors, laying bare the doors of a fourth shrine'.

Seal and cord (Carter no. 238a) on the third shrine (Carter no. 238); diameter of cord: 0.4 cm
Glass plate negative, 23.9 × 17.9 cm
Harry Burton, 3 January 1924
Burton P0631

238

24 POSED FOR DISCOVERY

The opening of the gilded shrines provided another opportunity to publicize the tomb across the world. Here, Carter (crouched), Callender (standing), and an unidentified Egyptian team member (foreground) are about to discover what lay inside the fourth shrine. But this image is not a simple objective view of a historic moment: here Burton photographed the men as a dramatically posed group, spotlit by a large electric lamp (positioned in the top corner of the shot), and with the shrine doors arranged so as to frame the view of Carter (motionless and sharply in focus) reaching towards the inner shrine. Another shot recorded the same actions in a much less artfully composed manner.

Opening the doors of the fourth shrine (Carter no. 239)
Glass plate negative, 23.9 × 17.9 cm
Harry Burton, 3 or 4 January 1924
Burton P0643

25 OPENED DOORS

Carter later described how, 'with intense excitement', on 3 January 1924 he 'drew back the bolts of the last and unsealed doors; they slowly swung open, and there, filling the entire area within, effectually barring any further progress, stood an immense yellow quartzite sarcophagus, intact, with the lid still firmly fixed in its place, just as the pious hands had left it'. This photograph shows the carved surface of one end of the sarcophagus seen through a sequence of opened doors, gilded door upon door. Another month of intense work would be needed to dismantle these shrines so that the team could reach the sarcophagus itself.

View through the shrines' doors; height of the door of the fourth shrine (Carter no. 239): 130 cm
Glass plate negative, 23.9 × 17.9 cm
Harry Burton, 4 January 1924
Burton P0644A

26 REMOVING A ROOF

In this atmospheric view of the Antechamber, Carter, two Egyptian colleagues and Callender lift up a section of the outer shrine's roof from the Burial chamber and insert wooden planks to support it. The ancient carpenters had created the gilded shrines in 'flatpack' form, ready to erect around the sarcophagus, and had written notes in ink on the various parts to help with the assembly. However, the space in the chamber proved so tight that they erected them facing in the opposite direction from what had been intended. Dismantling the shrines in this small tomb was perhaps even more of a challenge for Carter's team than the assembly had been for the ancient workers.

Dismantling the outer shrine (Carter no. 207)
Glass plate negative, 23.9 × 17.9 cm
Harry Burton, 16 December 1923
Burton P0605

27 BENEATH THE LID

Inside the shrines, a sarcophagus contained the king's coffins. In the photograph opposite, Burton created an intimate view of the outer coffin, evoking the stillness and silence of the tomb, with light falling on the king's face. Behind the sarcophagus are the dismantled and wrapped panels of the shrines. The royal forehead is still adorned with a tiny garland of cornflowers and olive leaves. During the burial, the end of the coffin's gilded foot had to be cut away as it was too big to allow the sarcophagus lid to close properly. This drastic alteration was made good with dark resin, which trickled down over the gilded coffin.

A garland on the royal insignia of cobra and vulture on the coffin's forehead; circumference of garland: 31 cm
Original print, 23.2 × 17.2 cm
Harry Burton, 5 February 1925
Burton P0709

Outer coffin (Carter no. 253) as found, inside the sarcophagus (Carter no. 240); dimensions of sarcophagus: 275 × 148 cm
Glass plate negative, 17.9 × 23.9 cm
Harry Burton, 5 February 1925
Burton P0705

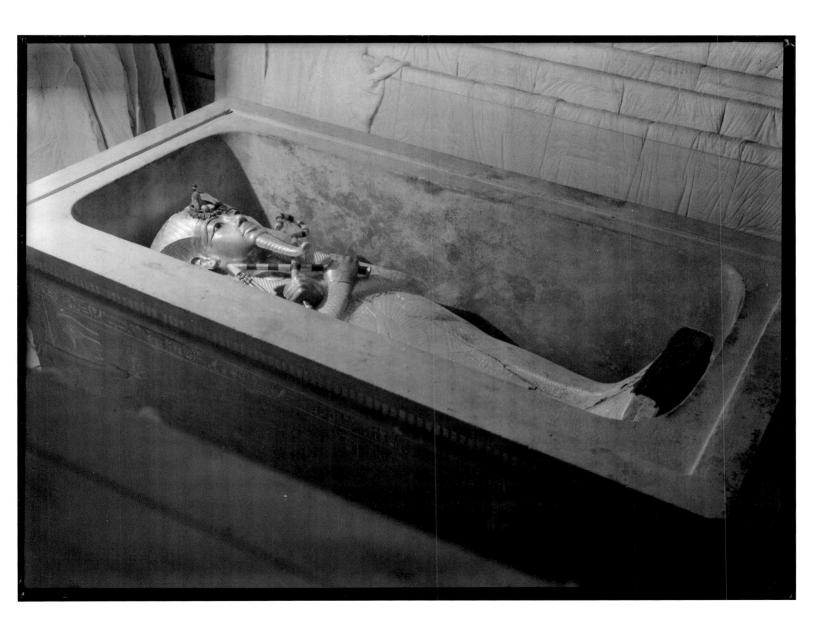

28 A VEIL WITH FLOWERS

This mysterious view of the king's middle coffin inside the sarcophagus captures a pause in the investigation, after the team lifted the lid of the outer coffin on 13 October 1925. The middle coffin is still enveloped in a linen shroud, draped with delicate garlands of cornflowers, blue lotus, and olive and willow leaves. Carter reflected that 'among all that regal splendour, … there was nothing so beautiful as those few withered flowers, still retaining their tinge of colour'. Once the photographic record was completed on 17 October, Carter 'carefully removed the wreath and garlands and was able to roll back the covering shroud' to reveal the richly decorated coffin beneath.

29 ARCHAEOLOGISTS AT WORK

During the funerary rituals, so much unguent was poured onto the third coffin that it not only covered the coffin's surface with a dark layer, but also glued it firmly to the middle coffin. Carter noted that the unguent's 'smell when warm was penetrating, somewhat fragrant, not unpleasant, and suggestive of wood pitch'. This staged photograph focuses on Carter's hand as he poses (motionless) in the Antechamber, removing the darkened remains of the shroud and unguents, while an Egyptian team member assists with a brush. Tools are conspicuously laid out on the wooden pallet to suggest the scientific nature of the examination. The composition also reveals the inequalities between the team members and their activities.

Howard Carter and an Egyptian colleague examining the inner coffin (Carter no. 255)
Original print, 17.2 × 23.2 cm
Harry Burton, probably 26 October 1925
Burton P0770

opposite **Upper part of the inner coffin (Carter no. 255) as found; width of coffin: 51.3 cm (max.)**
Replacement glass plate negative made from an original print (pinned to a board), 16.3 × 12 cm
Harry Burton, 24 October 1925
Burton P0731

30 A FLORAL COLLAR

In this shot, Burton's camera lens meets the enigmatic gaze of Tutankhamun's solid gold inner coffin wrapped in a reddish linen shroud. The coffin's face had been left uncovered in antiquity, with a folded cloth tucked between the head and the middle coffin (whose edges are covered with dark unguent). Around the neck is an elaborate broad floral collar (labelled as Carter no. 255a), made up of willow leaves, cornflowers, pomegranate leaves and nightshade berries with blue disc beads. The photograph captures the survival of the delicate plants but, as Carter later noted, 'although these at first appeared to be in good condition, they proved so brittle that the material broke the very instant it was touched'.

right **Lid of the inner coffin (Carter no. 255) after cleaning and waxing, laid on a black cloth and matting**
Glass plate negative, 23.9 × 17.9 cm
Harry Burton, probably shortly after 21 November 1925
Burton P0719C1

255

255.A.

opposite **Tutankhamun's funerary mask (Carter no. 256a); height: 54 cm**
Glass plate negative, 23.8 × 17.9 cm
Harry Burton, between 16 and 31 December 1925
Burton P0753

31   THE MASK

On the head of the king's mummified body was a mask of solid gold, richly inlaid, which has become the most iconic object from the tomb. Burton photographed it on a stand without its beard during the process of conservation, when the surfaces of the king's face and neck were dulled by a coat of paraffin wax, which was also a standard practice for photographing reflective objects. The resulting image shows the subtle modelling of the serene and eternally young face without the distractions of gold. For Carter, the mask bore a 'sad but tranquil expression' that he later said was 'suggestive of youth overtaken prematurely by death', appealing to a modern audience still mourning their own losses to war and epidemic.

right **View of the mask as found, an integral part of the mummified figure of the king (the mask is usually photographed as if it were an isolated portrait bust)**
Replacement glass plate negative made from original print, 16.3 × 12 cm
Harry Burton, 29 October 1925
Burton P0744

32 EXAMINING THE YOUNG KING

On 11 November 1925, a 'scientific examination' of the king's mummified body began in the conservation laboratory in the rock-cut tomb of Sety II, with the body still immovable in the inner coffin due to the funerary unguents (see no. 29). Burton captured the moment that the British surgeon Douglas Derry made the first incision into the mummy wrappings, watched by his Egyptian colleague Dr Saleh Bey Hamdi (on his right). Other onlookers include Carter and the French director-general of the Antiquities Service of Egypt, Pierre Lacau (1873–1963), while one of the Egyptian members of the official committee gazes back at the camera.

The official committee observing the first incision
Original print, 23.3 × 17.3 cm
Harry Burton, 11 November 1925
Burton P0939

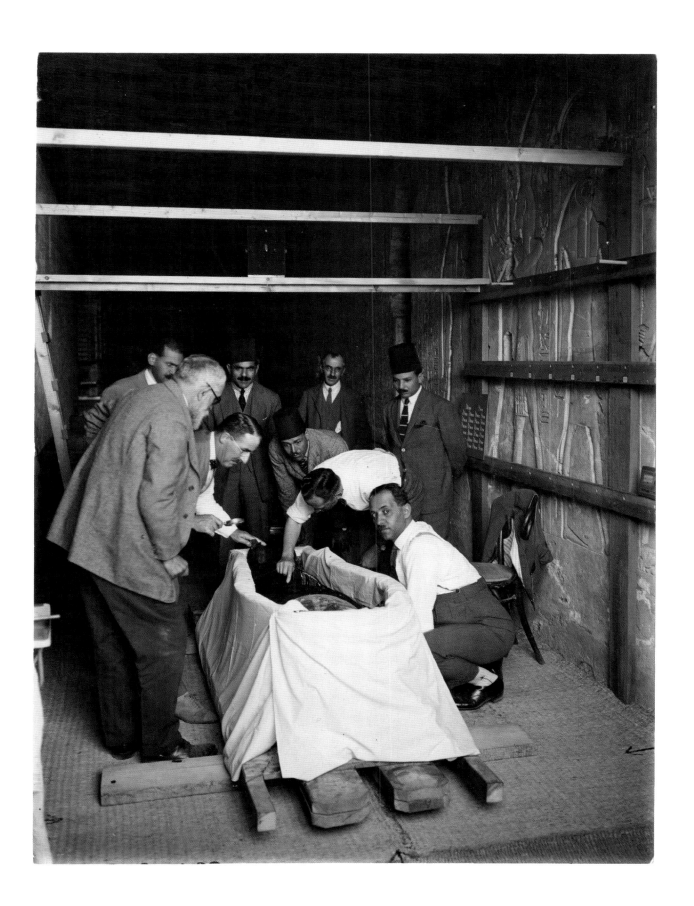

Drawing of the positions of the bracelets and rings on the king's forearms and hands, each numbered
Pencil on tracing paper, 25.7 × 20.6 cm
Howard Carter, between November 1925 and April 1926
TAA Archive i.4.10

33 THE KING'S JEWELLERY

The unwrapping and examination of the royal body took nine days, and some 150 amulets and other objects were discovered inside the layers of bandages. Burton photographed the position and appearance of each item, and in addition to the object cards for each (see no. 16), Carter later produced eighteen carefully finished illustrations of the king's body (the so-called 'autopsy drawings'). Six of these were published in *The Illustrated London News* on 26 February 1927. The drawing and the photograph here record the rings and the elaborate jewelled bracelets – over a dozen – that Tutankhamun wore on his bare forearms, which were folded on his chest. Above them, a broad collar of sheet gold is visible around his neck (labelled as Carter no. 256gg).

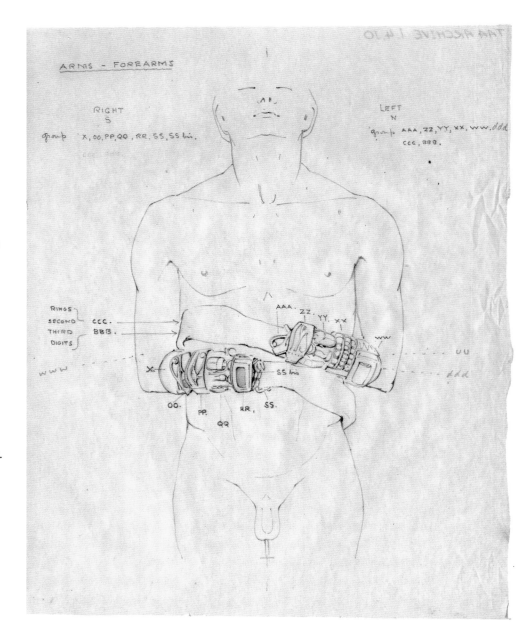

34 TWO VIEWS OF THE TREASURY

To the east of the Burial chamber was a storeroom, which Carter named the 'Treasury'. At the back of this room stood a tall, gilded shrine which Mace thought 'the most impressive monument I've ever seen'. This housed the king's embalmed internal organs which had accompanied his mummified body in the funerary procession. Placed in front, at the doorway, was a portable wooden shrine of the jackal god Anubis, still garlanded and draped with linen. These two images show Burton's artful use of light: in one, the room is seen lit from outside, but in the other, hidden lighting produces a highly dramatic and mysterious effect, spotlighting the spectacular shrine.

Two views of the Treasury; width of doorway: 112 cm
Glass plate negative, 23.9 x 17.9 cm; original print, 23.3 x 17.2 cm
Harry Burton, 24 October 1926
Burton P1169 (print) and 1169A

35 ANCIENT WRAPPINGS

Along one wall of the Treasury, there was a row of 'black, sinister, shrine-like chests ... all closed and sealed save one, the folding doors of which had fallen apart revealing statuettes of the king, swathed in linen, standing on the backs of black leopards'. Many of the objects in the tomb were found wrapped in linen, not just as packing material but as ritual coverings. These gilded statues were apparently intended to escort the king after death, and they were possibly deposited in the Treasury before the funeral took place. Model boats for use in the other world were stacked on either side, everything piled together in a complex process of deposition.

Shrine with two statuettes of the king on a panther (Carter no. 289); height of statues: 85.6 cm
Exchange print from Metropolitan Museum, 23.2 × 17.3 cm
Harry Burton, late October or early November 1926
Burton P1010B

36 A PACKED STOREROOM

The last room to be cleared by the team was a small storeroom (the Annexe) leading off the Antechamber, 'so packed one cannot see really what is there', and a 'witness of the neglect and dishonour that the royal tombs suffered'. The disarray made the clearance difficult for the team, who had to work suspended in a sling over the objects. This photograph records the southern end, already partially cleared and with the items numbered. The large triangular white box (Carter no. 370) was for the king's bows, arrows, throw sticks and clubs. The jumbled mass behind includes baskets, pots, decorative vessels (e.g. no. 579) and model boats (e.g. no. 437); on the top is an upturned bed (no. 377) and an upside-down white, child-sized throne (no. 349).

View of the Annexe during clearance; length of white box (Carter no. 370): 165.5 cm
Exchange print from Metropolitan Museum, 17.2 × 23.2 cm
Harry Burton, early December 1927
Burton P1689

37 PERFUME JARS

These ornate vessels, carved in translucent calcite, were found lined up between two of the ritual beds in the Antechamber (see no. 8). The jars with flanking elaborate heraldic plants, carved from a single piece of stone, once contained perfumed ointment. Ancient intruders damaged them, rifling them for the ointments: as this photograph shows, some vessels still had their lids in place when discovered, but one of them was balanced precariously on a broken stand. Its missing leg was found by the team elsewhere in the Antechamber, beside one of the 'guardian statues' – the official tidying after the attempted robbery had been hurried and incomplete.

Group of vessels in the Antechamber; height of front vessel (Carter no. 57): 52.9 cm
Glass plate negative, 23.8 × 17.9 cm
Harry Burton, between 18 and 24 December 1922
Burton P0010

38 A FEATHER FAN

One of the plain white boxes in the Treasury contained an elaborate rotating fan inscribed with the king's names. The only other contents were the dark desiccated remains of some persea fruit (top right). In this photograph, the fan's white and brown ostrich feathers look freshly plucked, and the gilded and decorated ivory handle still shows its polish. Of the nine fans found in the tomb, only this one still had its feathers, thanks to the protective box. Conservation with a spray including 'Duroprene' ensured the modern survival of these feathers which had once wafted the air in the royal court over 3,000 years earlier.

Box with fan (Carter no. 272); dimensions of box: 66.4 × 45.1 cm
Glass plate negative, 23.9 × 17.9 cm
Harry Burton, 5 November 1926
Burton P0997A

272

39 DETAILED DECORATION

The tomb contained six complete but dismantled chariots; four of these were found heaped in the Antechamber (see below). The photograph opposite shows a detail of the interior of the body of a gilded ceremonial chariot with extraordinarily rich decoration. The surface is covered with bands of spirals, rosettes and coloured inlays in a feather-like pattern, with a medallion containing a symbolic protective eye. An openwork copper-alloy attachment in the shape of a snake is set into the chariot body. The snake, its scales exquisitely detailed with gilding, is a hieroglyphic sign writing the word 'eternity'.

opposite **Chariot body (Carter no. 122) with a decorative serpent; length of serpent: 18 cm**
Glass plate negative, 16.3 × 12 cm
Harry Burton, early 1923
Burton P0540

below **View of the dismantled chariots (Carter nos 120–22, 161) piled unceremoniously beside the entrance to the tomb; diameter of uppermost wheel (Carter no. 122c): 93 cm (max.)**
Glass plate negative, 17.9 × 23.9 cm
Harry Burton, between 18 and 27 December 1922
Burton P0012

40 THE ROYAL WARDROBE

The textiles in the tomb ranged from pieces of everyday clothing to more elaborate state garments. Some of the gloves were quite small and must have been worn by the king as a child. Some were plain and perhaps intended to be worn when riding a chariot, but the example shown opposite was tapestry-woven in a red, blue and brown pattern, with tapes to secure it around the wrist; it was probably for ceremonial wear.

The tomb even preserved intimate undergarments – around 145 triangular pieces of linen to be wrapped around the waist from behind, with one end pulled up between the legs and all three corners tied together in front.

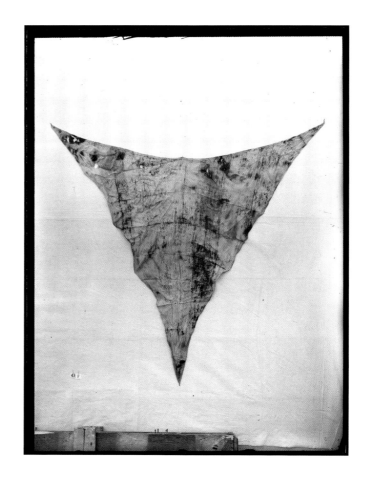

above **Linen loincloth (Carter no. 43f) from a box in the Antechamber; length of long edge: 135 cm**
Glass plate negative, 16.3 × 12 cm
Harry Burton, probably early 1923
Burton P0403

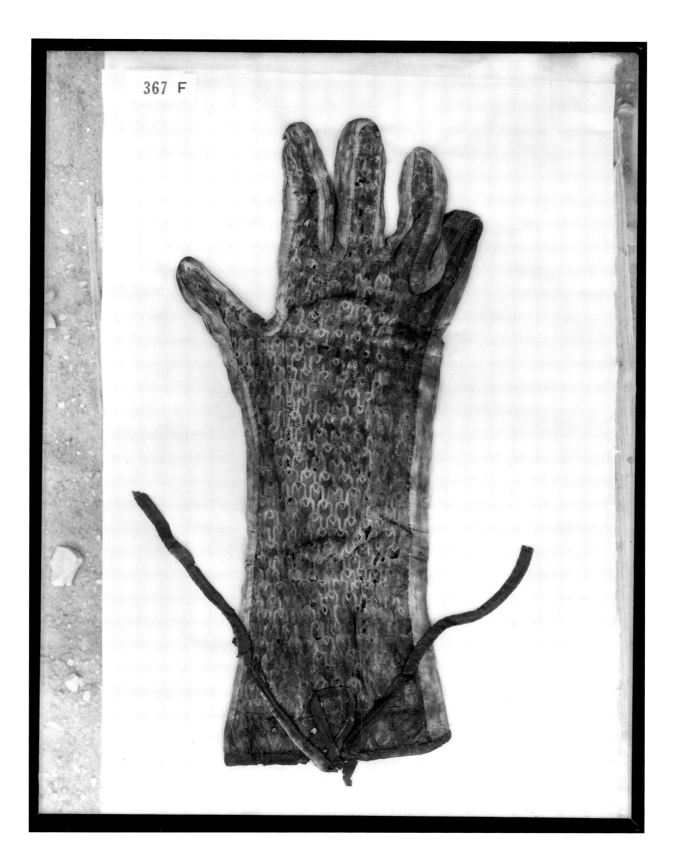

41 BASKETS AND ALBUMS

As well as chests and vases, a variety of finely woven baskets were placed in the tomb. Their contents included fruit, as with a large oval basket containing fruit of the dom palm, shown here with and without its lid (Carter no. 97). This is a page from a set of ten large albums of Burton's photographs, arranged in part by object type; Burton labelled each print with the negative number (top) and Carter's object number (bottom). The prints vary in size and tone, some being warmer and others more sepia, but all demonstrate a wide, smooth range of tone and very high definition of detail.

Photographic albums, half-bound in leather, produced by James Sinclair Company, London, with Burton prints
Leather, boards, paper, photographic prints, ink, 28 × 43 × 5.5 cm; album 9 is labelled 'LVIII–LXXXV'
Harry Burton, some time between 1924 and 1926
TAA Archive i.6.1–10

**Page of photographic album, half-bound in
leather, produced by James Sinclair Company,
London, with Burton prints (album 6, page 38)**
Leather, boards, paper, photographic prints, ink,
28 × 43 × 5.5 cm
TAA Archive i.6.6.38

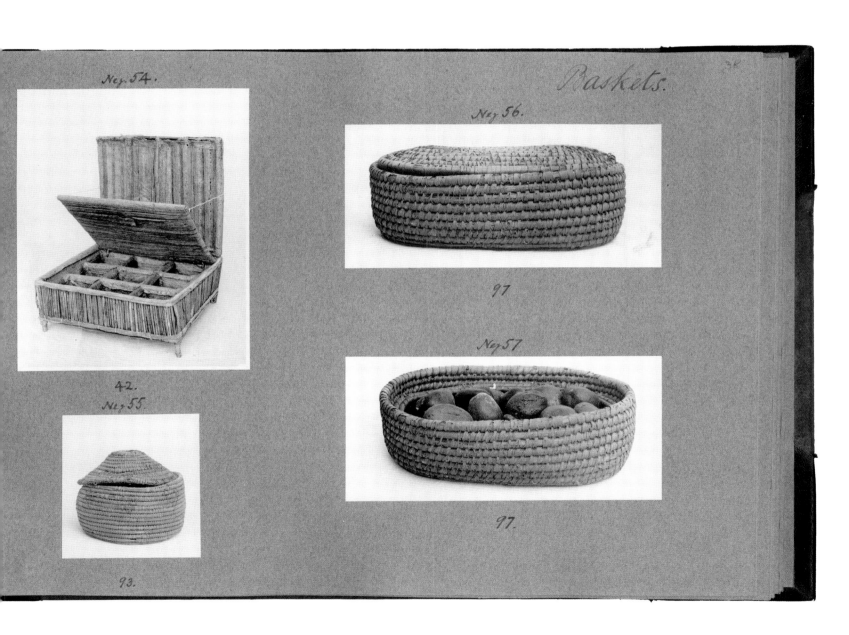

No. 54.

Baskets.

No. 56.

97

42.
No. 55.

No. 57

97.

93.

42 A STYLISH STOOL

Among the furniture in the tomb is what looks at first sight like a simple folding stool with a seat of cowhide, but it is made of ebony veneer and inlaid with ivory in an elegantly stylized imitation of a cowhide pattern, complete with a tail hanging down. The legs terminate in goose heads, with their beaks grasping the gilt-tipped foot bars (their tongues are even stained red). A travelling stool was transformed into something rich and exotic for the king. This is an example of the sort of photograph that Burton took to record individual objects, against a cloth backdrop and with a numbered card (Carter no. 83).

Ebony stool (Carter no. 83) from the Antechamber (found opposite the sealed doorway: see no. 8); height of stool: 34.5 cm
Glass plate negative, 12 × 16.3 cm
Harry Burton, probably early 1923
Burton P0353

83

43 ANCIENT AND MODERN

In this photograph an unnamed Egyptian boy wears a heavy jewelled necklace from a casket in the Treasury. Decades later, Hussein Abd el-Rassul of Gurna identified himself as the boy, and many stories have gathered around this evocative and moving image. When it was first published in *The Illustrated London News* in April 1927, the photograph was described as having been taken simply 'to show the method of suspension', but the boy's expression suggests a more complex human response and an awareness of the weight of ancient history on his shoulders. Here ancient and modern Egypt are seen together, the worlds of the living and the dead touching each other.

Egyptian boy wearing a pectoral (Carter no. 267g–h)
Glass plate negative, 23.9 × 17.9 cm
Harry Burton, late 1926 or early 1927
Burton P1189

44 THE PHOTOGRAPHER'S WIFE

Burton's wife Minnie accompanied him during his time working on the tomb. She kept a personal diary, which is now a valuable source of information about who was in Luxor during those busy years. Her entries recorded social engagements (numerous lunches, teas and dinners with fellow archaeologists, their families and eminent visitors), her regular walks and daily routines, taking care of the couple's living quarters, sewing, writing letters and gardening. Although she was not officially part of the team, she occasionally mentioned assisting her husband with the numbering and cataloguing of photographic prints. And here she records her first visit to 'the' tomb.

19 Dec. Tues.
Painting my furniture in morning & afternoon. M' Carter sent over for me his donkey to ride over & see "the" Tomb Tutankhamen. Wonderful. M' Callendar [sic] there & later D' & M'ˢ Breasted & the little girl. Went over the hill both ways. M' Hauser & Hall came back from Assuan. M'ˢ W[inlock] & F[rances] to the Davies' for tea.

Group photograph
Original print, 12.3 × 17.1 cm
Unknown photographer for the Metropolitan Museum's expedition, probably January 1925.
Davies MSS 12.9

This photograph of American and European archaeologists and their families was taken near the Metropolitan Museum's expedition house at Luxor, and includes Minnie (middle row, second from right) and Harry Burton (back row, third from right).

19 Dec. Painting my furniture in morning &
Tues. afternoon. Mr Carter sent over for me his
donkey to ride over & see "the" "Tomb"
Tutankhamen. Wonderful. Mr.
Callendar there & later Dr & Mrs
Breasted & the little girl. Went over
the hill both ways. Mr Hanson &
Hall came back from Assuan. Mrs
W. & F. to the Davies' for tea.

20 Dec. Walked Der-el-Bahari before tea & after &
Wed. to see Mrs Davies.

21 Dec. Painting Harry's chest of drawers. Before
Thurs. tea & top of cliff & met H & walked
back with him. Mrs Carter to dinner.

22 Dec. Bad night with coughing. Painting
Fri. bookshelves. Carpenter arranged my
shelves. Walk across cultivation with
Mrs Winlock between lunch & tea.
The Mc Aldines called while we
were out.

23 Dec. Painting my shelves & table most of
Sat. day. Harry's room colour-washed.

Miss Lattey, Mrs Hooker & Mrs Wright to
tea. Walked by Der el Bahari after & to
Mrs Davies'. Mrs W. seedy & not at dinner.
My green stuff arrived.

Dec 25. Gave Frances a Florentine leather
Xmas. bag. H. gave her a hat. I walked
twice round by Der el Bahari. Mrs
W. in bed all day. To dinner the
Davies', Mr. Wilkinson, Mr Carter
& Mr Lucas. Mr Mace arrived
in the morning. H not over to
Tombs.

26 Dec. H & I to Luxor to lunch with the
Tues. Contessa at the Luxor Hotel. Miss
Lattey & Mrs Wright also. To W.P. first
& saw Dr Deacon, Mr Davies, Mr
Englebach, Mc Aldines & Mellins.
Then shopping, & again afterwards
with the Contessa to Hassan's etc.
Tea at the Luxor. Mrs Hooker invited
us, but we refused. Dr Marsden &
his son) over to see Mrs Winlock who
is in bed with colitis. Back by moonlight.

Diary of Minnie C. Burton for 1922–6
Lined account book, bound in blue cloth, ink,
17.9 × 11 × 2.8 cm (closed)
Minnie C. Burton, Luxor, 19–26 December 1922
M. Burton Diary, pp. 64–5

45 THE TOURIST ATTRACTION

Tourists and journalists gathered around the tomb entrance to witness the world-famous 'treasures' being removed, even though they were often crated, like part of one of the ritual beds shown being carried out here. During the early months of the clearance crowds put the safe transport of the objects at risk, and the Egyptian government banned visits to the valley site without a special permit. Permission to enter the tomb, however, was often given to privileged individuals – generally royalty, dignitaries or academic colleagues. Issues about who was allowed access sparked a legal dispute between Carter and the Egyptian authorities that halted the work for almost a year in 1924–5.

Spectators watching an object (part of Carter no. 137) being removed from the tomb
Glass plate negative made from print, 8.2 × 10.7 cm
Unknown photographer (perhaps Arthur Merton from *The Times*), February 1923
TAA Archive ii.4.10

The discovery of the tomb created intense popular interest, and the team's work became a media sensation thanks to daily reporting by the international press. 'Tutmania' influenced all levels of popular culture (see no. 49). Carter responded to this fascination with a series of public lectures, including a punishing but financially rewarding tour to North America in 1924, as well as tours in Europe. He illustrated his lectures using a magic lantern and slides made from Burton's photographs, some of which were hand-tinted to convey the full effect of the objects to 'enthusiastic applause' in packed halls and theatres.

above **Lantern slide of a calcite lamp (Carter no. 173), lit from the inside; height of vessel: 51.4 cm (max.)**
Glass with paper mount, tape, labels and pencil,
8.2 × 8.2 × 0.3 cm
Hand-tinted positive by Reginald A. Malby & Co.,
probably 1925 or shortly after
Burton P0659B LS

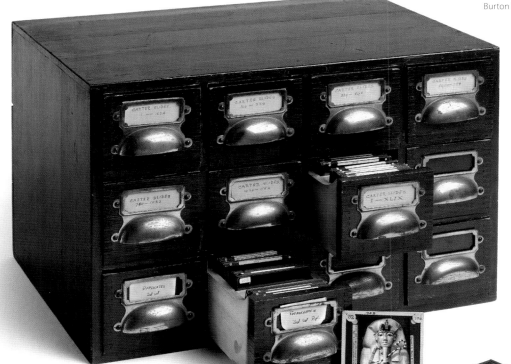

left **Howard Carter's twelve-drawered chest of over 600 glass lantern slides**
Wood with brass drawer handles, labels and ink,
31.7 × 48 × 36.7 cm
Unknown maker, early 1920s
TAA Archive i.8

47 FAN MAIL

The discovery touched many lives, and Carter was 'inundated with letters … [and] inquiries of every description' from an enthusiastic public around the world, especially in the first months after the discovery. These included letters of congratulation, offers of money for 'some little token taken direct from the tomb' and commercial proposals. One of the letters that was kept is this hand-crafted card sent by a six-year-old Irish boy who wanted to be 'an Egyptolisty like you'. His hieroglyphs include a rendering of one of Tutankhamun's names, and when Luke Dillon-Mahon (1917–1997) grew up he studied painting and became a notable artist, with a career in advertising.

from
Luke Mahon
Castlegar
Ahascragh
Ireland.
With best wishes for your <u>great</u> discovery.
I am wishing I was an Egyptolisty like you.
I am 6 now, praps I will be one when I am grown up. I love all about Tutenkamen.

Card from Luke Mahon to Howard Carter
Paper, ink, pencil, coloured paints and cotton cord; cover sheet: 17.3 × 22.7 cm (open)
Luke Mahon, undated, but probably late 1922 or early 1923
TAA Archive ii.3.14

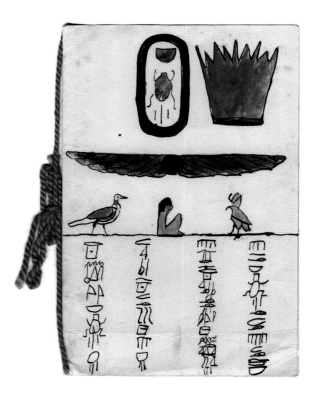

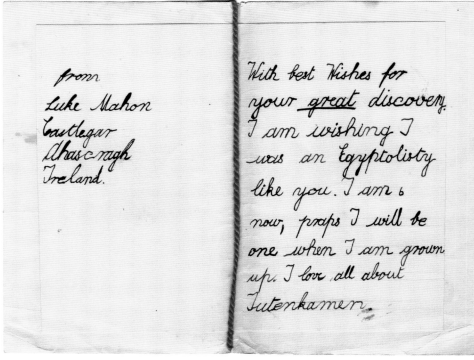

48 OCCULT ADVICE

Ancient Egypt was often associated with the occult in popular culture, and this anonymous telegram was sent from Dublin to 'Carter Tutenkamen Thebes' on 13 January 1923. It warns 'if trouble continues reseal tomb pour milk oil wine at threshold', probably inspired by a newspaper report on the previous day that a dust storm had halted work at the tomb. The sender was almost certainly Ella Young (1867–1956), an Irish poet and Celtic mythologist, who later wrote letters to Carter claiming that Carnarvon had died because 'the tomb of Tutankhamen was opened without any ceremonies calculated to placate any Ka [spirit] or Kas that might be in the sepulchre'.

Telegram addressed to Howard Carter
Paper, coloured pencil and ink, 14.8 × 25.4 cm
[Ella Young], 13 January 1923
TAA Archive ii.3.25

49 SELLING KING TUT

In the years of popular 'Tutmania', manufacturers produced every imaginable form of merchandise, often inspired by Burton's published photographs and the press reports. The centre of this American *Tutoom* board game is occupied by the enthroned king, and the board squares include scenes of archaeologists travelling through the desert towards the tomb. The game's counters are tiny archaeologists on donkeys, inspired by the team's actual daily mode of transport to and from the site. The rules are similar to those of Snakes and Ladders, and the aim is to be the first player to reach 'the treasures of pharaoh'.

***Tutoom: Journey to the Treasures of Pharaoh*
board game**
Printed board, with playing counters; board:
44.6 × 43.7 cm
Manufactured by Alderman, Fairchild Co.
Rochester, NY, USA, 1923
TAA Archive ii.3.25

50 A FINAL PHOTOGRAPH

During the 1932 Christmas dinner at the Metropolitan Museum's expedition house at Luxor, Carter informed Burton that, although their last season was ended, they had forgotten to photograph the sarcophagus fully. Assisted by Carter, Burton took his last set of photographs in the first days of 1933, and then was finally 'finished' with the tomb. They include this general view of the monumental sarcophagus, carved with protective goddesses at each corner, their winged arms stretched out to embrace the young king. Today, the sarcophagus still stands in the heart of the small tomb that safeguarded the royal burial with all its 'wonderful things'.

View of sarcophagus (Carter no. 240) in the Burial chamber; dimensions of sarcophagus: 275 × 148 × 148 cm
Glass plate negative, 17.9 × 23.9 cm
Harry Burton, mid-January 1933
Burton P0646F

WORK ON THE TOMB, SEASON BY SEASON

Season	Dates	Summary of activities
1ST	NOVEMBER 1922–MAY 1923	Discovery of tomb; clearance of the Antechamber; opening of the Burial chamber; death of Lord Carnarvon
2ND	OCTOBER 1923–FEBRUARY 1924	Work on last objects from the Antechamber; clearance of the Burial chamber; dismantling of the gilded shrines; lifting of the sarcophagus lid; dispute with Egyptian authorities
3RD	JANUARY–MARCH 1925	Work on objects from the Burial chamber; preparatory work on the outer coffin
4TH	OCTOBER 1925–MAY 1926	Opening of the coffins; uncovering of the gold mask; examination of the mummified body
5TH	OCTOBER 1926 TO APRIL 1927	Return of Tutankhamun's body to the sarcophagus; start of the clearance of the Treasury
6TH	SEPTEMBER 1927–APRIL 1928	Completion of the clearance of the Treasury; clearance of the Annexe
7TH	OCTOBER 1928–EARLY 1929	Conservation and photographic work on objects
8TH	WINTER OF 1929–30	No work; Carter negotiating with the Egyptian government about a financial settlement for the Carnarvon family
9TH	OCTOBER–NOVEMBER 1930	Removal of the dismantled shrines from the tomb; opening of the sealed niches in the Burial chamber
10TH	WINTER OF 1930–31	Conservation work on the shrines
11TH	WINTER OF 1931–2	Further work on the shrines and shipment to Cairo
	WINTER OF 1932–3	Photography of the reassembled shrines in the Egyptian Museum Cairo and of the sarcophagus in the tomb

Numbers in brackets refer to the records in this book.

1922	1 NOVEMBER	Start of the excavation season in the Valley of the Kings [4]
	4 NOVEMBER	Discovery of the steps [5–6]
	5 NOVEMBER	Sealed doorway of the tomb uncovered
	23 NOVEMBER	Lord Carnarvon arrives in Luxor [3]
	25 NOVEMBER	Opening of the first sealed doorway
	26 NOVEMBER	Opening of the second doorway [7–9]
	29 NOVEMBER	Official opening of the tomb
	27 DECEMBER	Clearance of the Antechamber begins (completed mid-February 1923) [11–18, 37, 39, 41–2, 44–5]
1923	16 FEBRUARY	Opening of the Burial chamber [20–21; see also 47–9]
	5 APRIL	Lord Carnarvon dies in Cairo
	14 MAY	First crates with objects leave for the Egyptian Museum Cairo (arriving 22 May) [19]
1924	3 JANUARY	Opening of the shrines; the sarcophagus is revealed [23–6]
	12 FEBRUARY	Lifting of the sarcophagus lid [27]
	12 APRIL	Carter sets off on lecture tour in the USA and Canada (until 2 July) [46]
1925	13 OCTOBER	Removal of the lid of the outer coffin [28]
	23 OCTOBER	Removal of the lid of the middle coffin [29–30]
	28 OCTOBER	Removal of the lid of the inner coffin, revealing the gold mask and mummified body [31]
	11 NOVEMBER	Examination of the mummified body begins (completed 19 November) [32–3]

TIMELINE

1926	23 OCTOBER	Reburial of the king's body in the sarcophagus inside the tomb
	24 OCTOBER	Start of work in the Treasury (completed in November 1927) [34–5, 38, 43]
1927	30 NOVEMBER	Start of work in the Annexe (completed 15 December) [36, 40]
1930	3 NOVEMBER	Niche in Burial chamber opened [10, 22]
	10 NOVEMBER	Dismantled shrines removed from the tomb
1932	1 FEBRUARY	Final objects (the dismantled shrines) shipped to Cairo
1933	MID-JANUARY	Final photographs taken of the sarcophagus [50]
1939	2 MARCH	Howard Carter dies in London
	26 AUGUST	First batch of the Tutankhamun archive is transported from London to Oxford, placed on 'protective deposit' in the Ashmolean Museum; donated to the Griffith Institute on 10 May 1945 by Phyllis Walker
1940	27 JUNE	Harry Burton dies in Asyut, Egypt
1946	EARLY MAY	Carter's set of Burton glass plate negatives and prints transported from London to the Griffith Institute
1955		Carter's maps and plans for the tomb of Tutankhamun, together with his earlier excavation work in the Valley of the Kings and other sites in Egypt, donated to the Griffith Institute by the Metropolitan Museum of Art in New York

A GUIDE TO THE ARCHIVE

Records connected with Tutankhamun's tomb in the archive of the Griffith Institute are prefixed by TAA (TutAnkhAmun):

TAA i   excavation records by Howard Carter, primary material

TAA ii   material other than excavation records, such as a folder of mail addressed to Carter that was dealt with by Mace, e.g. nos 47–8

TAA iii   secondary material

TAA iv   primary material on loan to the Griffith Institute, such as Mace's account of the opening of the Burial chamber (see no. 20)

Other papers of Howard Carter which are not connected with the tomb of Tutankhamun are catalogued in the archive as Carter MSS (e.g. no. 4). Papers of other individuals are designated in a similar way, such as Davies MSS, Gardiner MSS, Petrie MSS, Ross photographs, and Griffith Institute Watercolours and Drawings.

The images classified as 'Burton' are prefixed with the letter P (for 'photograph'). The majority of the images in this group were taken by Burton but some were taken by others (e.g. no. 6). They exist in various forms as glass plate negatives, copy negatives and/or as prints (both original and modern). The letters 'LS' are used to denote 'lantern slides' made from the images (e.g. no. 46). Burton and Carter also took over ninety photographs of the Valley of the Kings landscape including exterior views of Tutankhamun's tomb and related activities (e.g. no. 19); originally a Roman numeral sequence distinguished these images from the main excavation photograph numbers, but they are now referred to with Arabic numbers prefixed by KV (Kings Valley).

Often there is no date recorded for the photographs and drawings (e.g. nos 3, 6), and dates have to be deduced from surviving accounts of the team's activities, such as Carter's journals and diaries, which can be compared with the items and events shown in the images themselves. We have tried to be as specific as possible, but often only a possible range of dates is indicated.

The Griffith Institute's archive is accessible online at www.griffith.ox.ac.uk/archive and https://archive.griffith.ox.ac.uk/index.php. The material relating to Tutankhamun can be viewed on the website Tutankhamun: Anatomy of an Excavation, www.griffith.ox.ac.uk/discoveringTut. These pages include the list of objects from the tomb as numbered by Carter, with scans and transcriptions of the 3,500 object cards. As well as the original Carter numbers, the objects from the tomb also have numbers assigned by the Egyptian Museum in Cairo, exhibition numbers (listed online with the Carter numbers) and a new set of numbers in the Grand Egyptian Museum. The site also presents the Burton photographs for the excavation, a timeline for Howard Carter's Excavation journals and diaries with transcripts and images, Carter's notes and drawings made for the planned full publication of the tomb, related maps and plans, the conservation records created by Alfred Lucas, alternative accounts of the discovery and clearance, and material relating to Carter's earlier work.

NOTES TO THE INTRODUCTION

1. For an account of the funeral see Marianne Eaton-Krauss, *The Unknown Tutankhamun*, Bloomsbury, London, 2016, pp. 103–18.

2. Wolfgang Helck, *Urkunden der 18. Dynastie*, no. 22, Akademie-Verlag, Berlin, 1958, p. 2027 (author's translation).

3. Quotations are from: a label on a box (Carter no. 68: Jaroslav Černý, *Hieratic Inscriptions from the Tomb of Tut'ankhamūn*, Tut'ankhamūn's Tomb Series 2, Griffith Institute, Oxford, 1965, pp. 9–10, 26 (no. 50)); a hieroglyphic inscription on a walking stick (Carter no. 229: Horst Beinlich and Mohamed Saleh, *Corpus der hieroglyphischen Inschriften aus dem Grab des Tutanchamun*, Griffith Institute, Oxford, 1989, p. 67).

4. Harry Burton, quoted in T.G.H. James, *Howard Carter: The Path to Tutankhamun*, rev. paperback edn Taurus Parke, London, 2001, p. 277.

5. Letter of Lord Carnarvon to Alan Gardiner, 28 November 1922: Gardiner MSS, Newspaper Cuttings Album, 1.39.1 (no. 9), Griffith Institute archive.

6. E.M. Forster, 'The Objects', *The Athenaeum*, no. 4697, 7 May 1920, pp. 599–600. Reprinted as 'For the Museum's Sake' in E.M. Forster, *Abinger Harvest*, E. Arnold, London, 1936, pp. 280–6.

7. Tennessee Williams, *The Night of the Iguana*, act 3, in *Cat on a Hot Tin Roof; The Milk Train Doesn't Stop Here Anymore; The Night of the Iguana*, Penguin Books, London, 1976, p. 324.

8. Letter of Albert M. Lythgoe to Edward Robinson, 20 December 1922, quoted in James, *Howard Carter: The Path to Tutankhamun*, p. 270.

9. See Howard Carter, *The Tomb of Tut.ankh.Amen: Discovered by the Late Earl of Carnarvon and Howard Carter*, 3 vols, Cassell, London, 1923–33, vol. 1, pp. xv–xvi, vol. 2, p. xxiv.

10. Christina Riggs, *Photographing Tutankhamun: Archaeology, Ancient Egypt, and the Archive*, Bloomsbury, London, 2019, p. 3.

11. *Daily Express*, 10 February 1923, in Percy Newberry's Album of newspaper cuttings, NEWB1/12.17, Griffith Institute archive.

12. Elliott Colla, *Conflicted Antiquities: Egyptology, Egyptomania, Egyptian Modernity*, Duke University Press, Durham, NC, and London, 2007, p. 206.

13. *Al Ahram*, 31 January 1923, p. 1 (translation by Hebatallah Ibrahim).

14. See Riggs, *Photographing Tutankhamun*, pp. 48–53.

15. Letter of Phyllis Walker to Alan Gardiner, 10 May 1945: Carter MSS, TAA Archive Accession Correspondence, file 1945.

16. See e.g. Eleanor Dobson, *Writing the Sphinx: Literature, Culture and Egyptology*, Edinburgh Critical Studies in Victorian Culture, Edinburgh University Press, Edinburgh, 2020, pp. 21–3.

17. Christina Riggs, 'Water Boys and Wishful Thinking', *Photographing Tutankhamun* [blog], 2020, https://photographing-tutankhamun.com/2020/06/20/the-water-boy-who-wasnt (accessed 7 June 2021).

18. From 'Tut Ankh Amun wa-hadarat 'asrih', quoted in Colla, *Conflicted Antiquities*, p. 217.

SOURCES OF QUOTATIONS IN THE RECORDS

2   'we all inherited …': Howard Carter, 'Autobiographical Sketches', Carter MSS vi.2.9.1.

3   'Lord C.': a term used, for example, in Howard Carter's Excavation journal for 8 November 1922, TAA Archive i.2.1.29.

7   'Great Moment': letter of Lady Evelyn Herbert to Howard Carter, 26 December 1922, quoted in T.G.H. James, *Howard Carter: The Path to Tutankhamun*, rev. paperback edn, Taurus Parke, London, 2001, p. 464.

     'when Lord Carnarvon …': Howard Carter, *The Tomb of Tut.ankh.Amen: Discovered by the Late Earl of Carnarvon and Howard Carter*, 3 vols, Cassell, London, 1923–33, vol. i, pp. 94–6.

8   'gilded couches …'; 'a heap of large …': Excavation journal for 26 November 1922, TAA Archive i.2.1.35 (see pp. 40–41).

18 'not one-tenth …': Carter, *The Tomb of Tut.ankh. Amen*, vol. iii, p. 152.

20 'as though set …', 'each person …': Mace's account of 3 March 1923, TAA Archive iv.1.3 (reproduced with permission of the Orr family).

     Gardiner's letter to his wife, Gardiner MSS 47.08.6.

23 'cut the cords …': Excavation journal for 3 January 1924, TAA Archive i.2.1.101.

25 'with intense excitement …': Carter, *The Tomb of Tut. ankh.Amen*, vol. i, p. 45.

28 'among all that regal splendour …': Carter, *The Tomb of Tut.ankh.Amen*, vol. ii, p. 53.

     'carefully removed …': Excavation journal for 17 October 1925, TAA Archive i.2.3.19.

29 'smell when warm …': Carter, *The Tomb of Tut.ankh. Amen,* vol. ii, p. 81.

30 'although these at first …': Carter, *The Tomb of Tut. ankh.Amen*, vol. ii, p. 79.

31 'sad but tranquil …': Excavation journal for 28 October 1925, TAA Archive i.2.3.41. 'suggestive of youth …': Carter, *The Tomb of Tut.ankh.Amen*, vol. ii, p. 83.

32 'scientific examination': Excavation journal for 1 October 1925, TAA Archive i.2.3.1.

34 'the most impressive …': Mace's account of 3 March 1923, TAA Archive iv.1.4 (reproduced with permission of the Orr family).

35 'black, sinister …': Carter, *The Tomb of Tut.ankh. Amen*, vol. iii, p. 33.

36 'so packed …': letter from Lord Carnarvon to Alan Gardiner, 28 November 1922 (undated), Gardiner MSS, Newspaper Cuttings Album, 1.39.1 (see pp. 44–5).

     'Witness of the neglect …': Carter, *The Tomb of Tut. ankh.Amen*, vol. iii, p. 99 (original MS, TAA Archive i.2.10).

43 'to show the method …': *The Illustrated London News*, 23 April 1927, p. 726.

46 'enthusiastic applause': *The Times*, 22 September 1923, p. 8.

47 'inundated with letters …': *The Times*, 19 January 1923, p. 10.

     'some little token …': letter from C. Foster Hayes, Imperial Laboratories, Kansas City, MO, 17 February 1923, TAA Archive ii.3.7.

48 'the tomb …': letter from Ella Young to Howard Carter, 8 April 1923, TAA Archive ii.3.23.

50 'finished': letter from Harry Burton to H.E. Winlock, 20 January 1933, quoted in C. Riggs, *Photographing Tutankhamun: Archaeology, Ancient Egypt, and the Archive*, Bloomsbury, London, 2019, p. 31 (MMA/HB: 1930–35).

FURTHER READING

Allen, S.J., *Tutankhamun's Tomb: The Thrill of Discovery*, photographs by Harry Burton, Metropolitan Museum of Art, Yale University Press, New Haven and London, 2006.

Carter, H., *The Tomb of Tut.ankh.Amen: Discovered by the Late Earl of Carnarvon and Howard Carter*, 3 vols, Cassell, London, 1923–33.

Colla, E., *Conflicted Antiquities: Egyptology, Egyptomania, Egyptian Modernity*, Duke University Press, Durham, NC, and London, 2007.

Collins, P., and L. McNamara, *Discovering Tutankhamun*, Ashmolean Museum, Oxford, 2014.

Connor, S., and D. Laboury (eds), *Tutankhamun: Discovering the Forgotten Pharaoh, Exhibition Organized at the Europa Expo Space TGV Train Station 'Les Guillemins', Liège, 14th December 2019–30th August 2020*, Ægyptiaca Leodiensia 12, Presses Universitaires de Liège, Liège, 2020.

Daudy, K., *I Am Easy to Find* [artist's response to *Tutankhamun: Treasures of the Lost Pharaoh*, Saatchi Gallery], Kate Daudy Studio, London, 2020.

Dobson, E., '"Wonderful Things": Howard Carter, Literary Genre and Material Intertextuality', in *Writing the Sphinx: Literature, Culture and Egyptology*, Edinburgh Critical Studies in Victorian Culture, Edinburgh University Press, Edinburgh, 2020, pp. 21–58.

Eaton-Krauss, M., 'Publications in Monographic Form of the "Treasure" of Tutankhamun, 1952–2020', *Göttinger Miszellen*, vol. 262, 2021, pp. 217–25.

Eaton-Krauss, M., 'Tutankhamun's Tomb and "Treasure," 1922–1939', in press.

Eaton-Krauss, M., *The Unknown Tutankhamun*, Bloomsbury, London, 2016.

Hawass, Z., *King Tutankhamun: The Treasures of the Tomb*, photographs by Sandro Vannini, Thames & Hudson, London, 2007.

Ikram, S., 'An Epistolary Footnote: Howard Carter, Saleh Hamdi Bey, and Tutankhamun's Mummy', in Martina Ullmann, Gabriele Pieke, Friedhelm Hoffmann and Christian Bayer (eds), *Up and Down the Nile: Ägyptologische Studien für Regine Schulz*, Ägypten und Altes Testament 97, Zaphron, Münster, 2021, pp. 205–8.

James, T.G.H., *Howard Carter: The Path to Tutankhamun*, rev. paperback edn, Taurus Parke, London, 2001.

Malek, J., *The Treasures of Tutankhamun*, Andre Deutsch, London, 2006.

Reeves, N., *The Complete Tutankhamun: The King, the Tomb, the Royal Treasure*, Thames & Hudson, London, 1990.

Reeves, N., and J.H. Taylor, *Howard Carter before Tutankhamun*, British Museum Press, London, 1990.

Reid, D.M., *Contesting Antiquity in Egypt: Archaeologies, Museums and the Struggle for Identities from World War I to Nasser*, American University in Cairo Press, Cairo, 2015.

Reid, D.M., 'Remembering and Forgetting Tutankhamun: Imperial and National Rhythms of Archaeology, 1922–1972', in William Carruthers (ed.), *Histories of Egyptology: Interdisciplinary Measures*, Routledge, London and New York, 2015, pp. 157–73.

Riggs, C., 'Photography and Antiquity in the Archive, or How Howard Carter Moved the Road to the Valley of the Kings', *History of Photography*, vol. 40, no. 3, 2016, pp. 267–82.

Riggs, C., *Photographing Tutankhamun: Archaeology, Ancient Egypt, and the Archive*, Bloomsbury, London, 2019.

Riggs, C., 'Photographing Tutankhamun: Photo-Objects and the Archival Afterlives of Colonial Archaeology', in Julia Bärnighausen, Costanza Caraffa, Stefanie Klamm, Franka Schneider and Petra Wodtke (eds), *PhotoObjects: On the Materiality of Photographs and Photo Archives in the Humanities and Sciences*, Max Planck Research Library 12, Max Planck Gesellschaft zur Förderung der Wissenschaften, Berlin, 2020, pp. 291–308.

Riggs, C., *Tutankhamun: The Original Photographs*, Rupert Wace Ancient Art, London, 2017.

Roehrig, C.H. and M. Daniel, 'Harry Burton (1879–1940): The Pharaoh's Photographer', in *Heilbrunn Timeline of Art History*, The Metropolitan Museum of Art, New York, 2009, www.metmuseum.org/toah/hd/harr/hd_harr.htm.

Winstone, H.V.F. 1991, *Howard Carter and the Discovery of the Tomb of Tutankhamun*, Constable, London, 1991.

Publications of the tomb of Tutankhamun by the Griffith Institute, Oxford

Beinlich, H., and M. Saleh, *Corpus der hieroglyphischen Inschriften aus dem Grab des Tutanchamun*, 1989.

Černý, J., *Hieratic Inscriptions from the Tomb of Tutʿankhamūn*, Tutʿankhamūn's Tomb Series 2, 1965.

Davies, N.M., and A.H. Gardiner, *Tutankhamun's Painted Box*, 1962.

Eaton-Krauss, M., *The Sarcophagus in the Tomb of Tutankhamun*, 1993.

Eaton-Krauss, M., *The Thrones, Chairs, Stools, and Footstools from the Tomb of Tutankhamun*, 2008.

Eaton-Krauss, M., and E. Graefe, *The Small Golden Shrine from the Tomb of Tutankhamun*, 1985.

El-Khouli, A.A.-R.H., R. Holthoer, C.A. Hope and O.E. Kaper, *Stone Vessels, Pottery, and Sealings from the Tomb of Tutʿankhamūn*, 1994.

Jones, D., *Model Boats from the Tomb of Tutʿankhamūn*, Tutʿankhamūn's Tomb Series 9, 1990.

Leek, F. F., *The Human Remains from the Tomb of Tutʿankhamūn*, Tutʿankhamūn's Tomb Series 5, 1972.

Littauer, M.A., and J.H. Crouwel, *Chariots and Related Equipment from the Tomb of Tutʿankhamūn*, Tutʿankhamūn's Tomb Series 8, 1985.

Manniche, L., *Musical Instruments from the Tomb of Tutʿankhamūn*, Tutʿankhamūn's Tomb Series 6, 1976.

Manniche, L., *The Ornamental Calcite Vessels from the Tomb of Tutankhamun*, 2019.

McLeod, W., *Composite Bows from the Tomb of Tutʿankhamūn*, Tutʿankhamūn's Tomb Series 3, 1970.

McLeod, W., *Self Bows and Other Archery Tackle from the Tomb of Tutʿankhamūn*, Tutʿankhamūn's Tomb Series 4, 1982.

Murray, H., and M. Nuttall, *A Handlist of Howard Carter's Catalogue of Objects in Tutʿankhamūn's Tomb*, Tutʿankhamūn's Tomb Series 1, 1963.

Tait, W.J., *Game-Boxes and Accessories from the Tomb of Tutankhamun*, Tutʿankhamūn's Tomb Series 7, 1982.

INDEX

References to illustrations are in italics

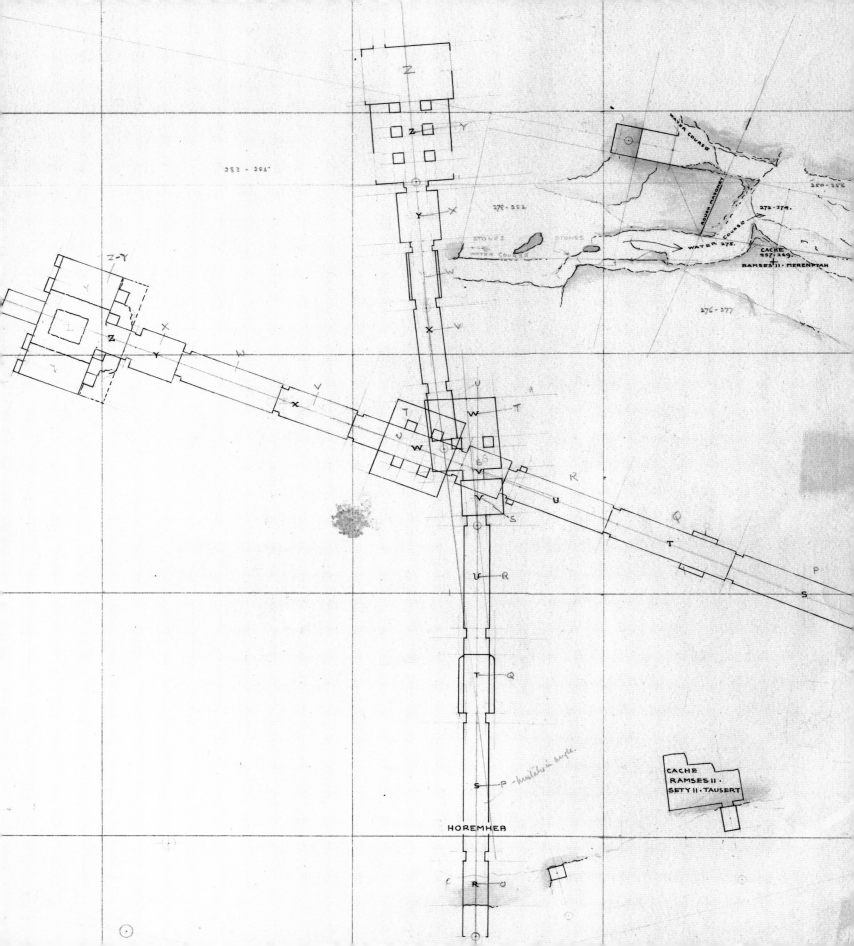

283 - 295

Z

Z

Y

Z - Y

Y

X

Z

Y

X

W

276 - 282

WATER COURSE

SOUTH MASONRY

272 - 274.

250 - 256

STONES   STONES

WATER COURSE

WATER 275.

CACHE
257 - 269.

RAMSES II · MERENPTAH

276 - 277

W

X   V

X   V

U   A

V

X

W   T

T

V

W

B

S   T

S

V

R

V   V   S

U

Q

T

V   R

P

S

T   Q

CACHE
RAMSES II ·
SETY II · TAUSERT

S   P — hatched-in angle.

HOREMHEB

R   U

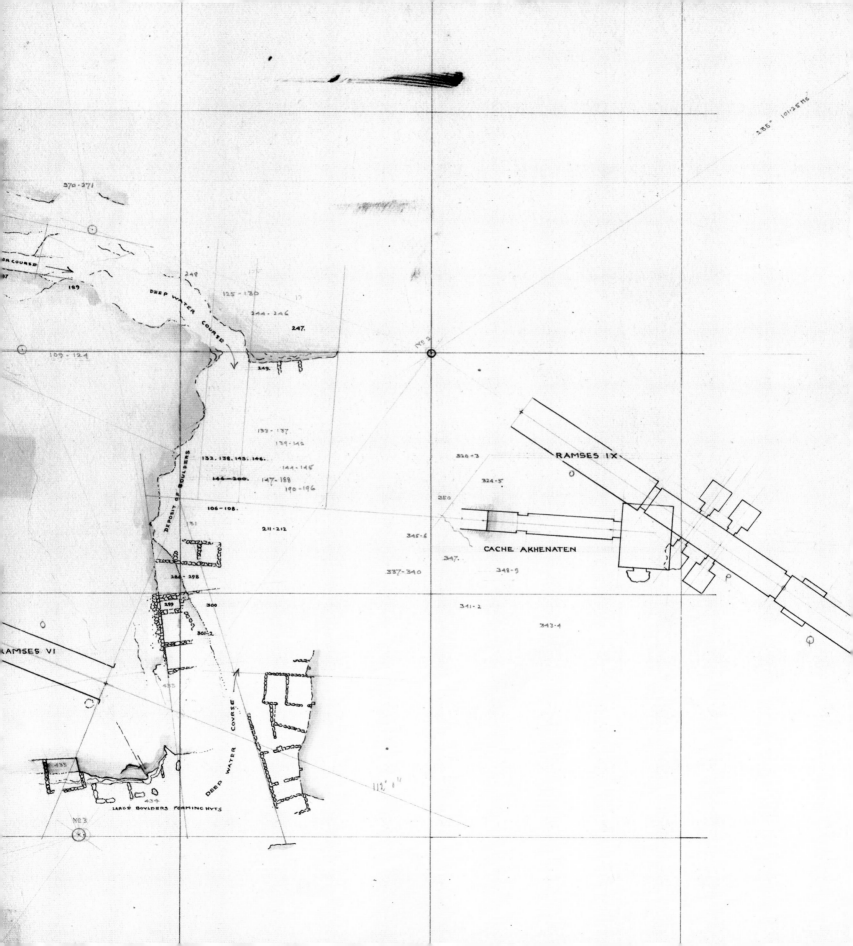

270-271

189

BR COURSE

97

DEEP WATER COURSE

248

125-130

244-246

247.

109-124

249.

133-137

139-142

132.138.143.146.

146-200.

144-145

147-188

190-196

106-108.

211-212

DEPOSIT OF BOULDERS

131

286-298

299

300

301-2

RAMSES VI

433

435

434

LARGE BOULDERS FORMING HUTS

DEEP WATER COURSE

No 3

235° 101·25 ms

320-3

RAMSES IX

324-5

O

350

345-6

CACHE AKHENATEN

347.

337-340

348-9

311-2

343-4

O

P

Q

112° 0"

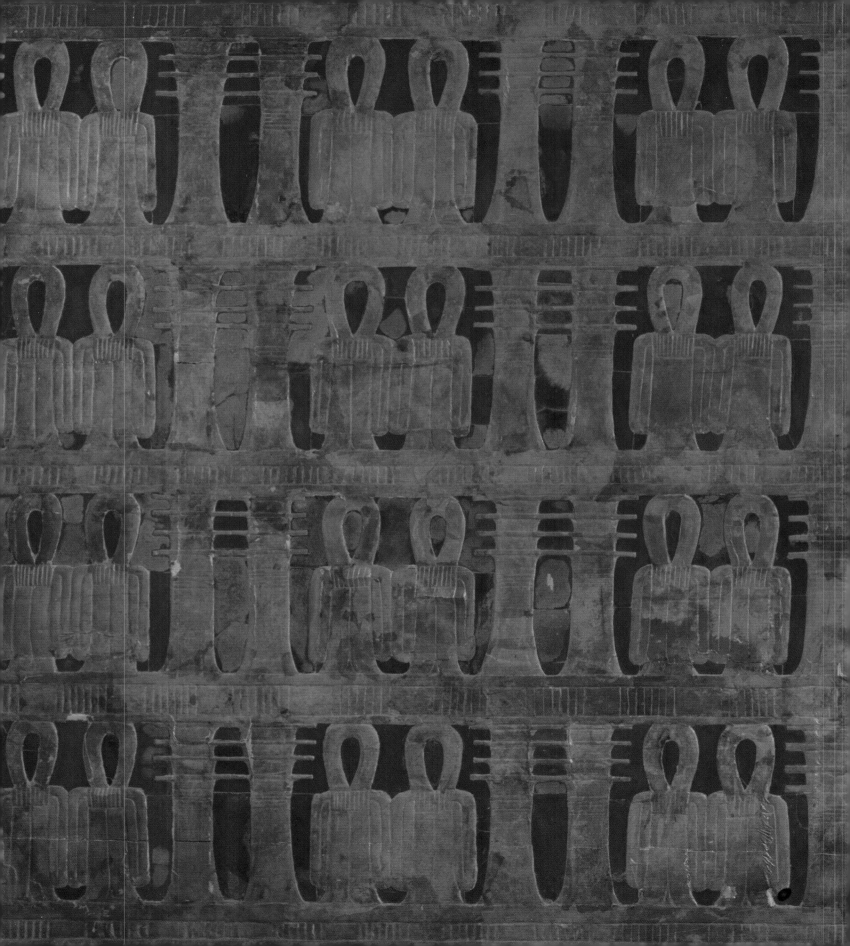

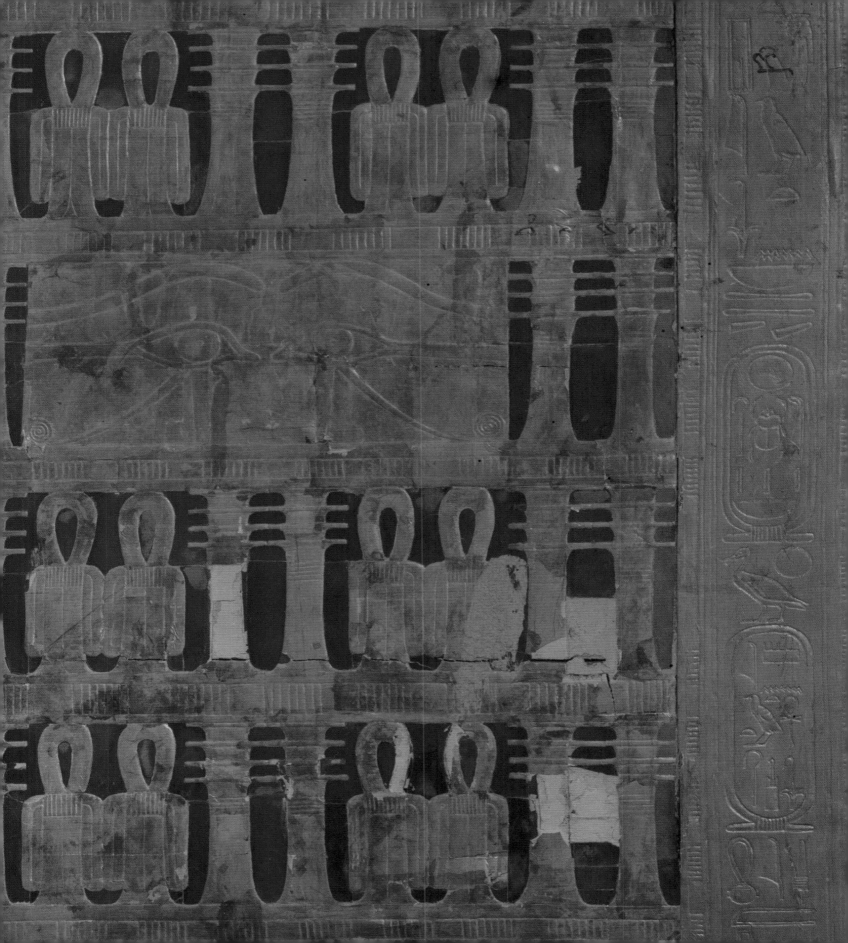

BODLEIAN
LIBRARY
PUBLISHING

The Griffith
INSTITUTE

First published in 2022 by the Bodleian Library
Broad Street, Oxford OX1 3BG
www.bodleianshop.co.uk

ISBN: 978 1 85124 585 7

Front cover: Garland on the forehead of the outer coffin, 5 February 1925. Burton P0709
Back cover: Opening the doors of the fourth shrine, 3 or 4 January 1924. Burton P0643
Endpapers: Object card by Howard Carter showing the statue of Anubis (see pp. 98–9),
1927. TAA Archive i.1.261.1
Frontispiece: View along the corridor into the tomb of Tutankhamun,
after electric lights and a security door had been installed, in
mid-December 1922. Burton P0005
page 6: The goddess Selket protecting the king with her wings,
carved on the sarcophagus (Carter no. 240). Burton P0646H

Publisher: Samuel Fanous
Managing Editor: Deborah Susman
Editor: Janet Phillips
Picture Editor: Leanda Shrimpton
Production Editor: Susie Foster
Designed and typeset by Dot Little at the Bodleian Library
in 10.5/15 Adobe Garamond
Printed and bound by Printer Trento S.r.l. on 150gsm Gardamatt Art paper

MIX
Paper from
responsible sources
FSC® C015829

British Library Catalogue in Publishing Data
A CIP record of this publication is available from the British Library

ANUBIS

POSITION: Placed in Centre of Chamber, partially
west. Ends of Carrying-poles of Shrine pro
into the Burial Chamber (See note attach

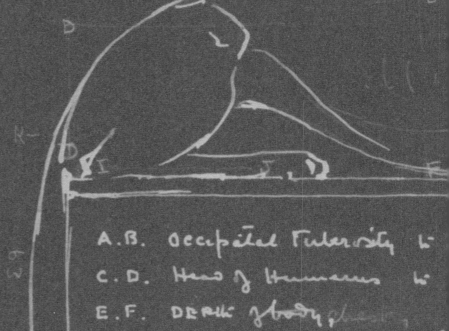

DIMENSIONS: Anubis
               Jackal

A.B. Occipital Tuberosity t
C.D. Head of Humerus t
E.F. Depth of body
G.H. Point of Elbow (olecranon)
I.J. Calcaneum to end of M
K.L. length of tail.